Practical English Handbook

Practical

**Houghton Mifflin Company
Boston**

*Atlanta
Dallas
Geneva, Illinois
Hopewell, New Jersey
Palo Alto
London*

English Handbook

Floyd C. Watkins
Emory University

William B. Dillingham
Emory University

Edwin T. Martin

Fourth Edition

PE
1408
W37

71020

Acknowledgment is made to the following sources of reprinted materials,
alphabetically listed by authors.

From Ruth Adam, "Smalltown America." Reprinted from *The Illustrated
London News*, May 1962.

From Francis R. Allen, *Socio-cultural Dynamics: An Introduction to Social
Change.* Copyright © 1971. Adapted for the exercise by permission of The
Macmillan Company.

From Frederick Lewis Allen, "The Road to Riches." Reprinted from the
Saturday Review of Literature, September 17, 1938; by permission.

From William O. Aydelotte, "The Detective Story as a Historical Source."
Reprinted from *The Yale Review*; by permission. Copyright 1949 Yale University Press.

From Charles S. Brooks, "On the Difference Between Wit and Humor," in
Chimney Pot Papers; reprinted by permission of Yale University Press.

From Harvey Cox, *The Secular City: Secularization and Urbanization in
Theological Perspective*, rev. ed. (New York: The Macmillan Company, 1966).

From Alexander DeConde, *Half Bitter, Half Sweet: An Excursion into
Italian-American History* (New York: Charles Scribner's Sons, 1972).
Adapted for the exercise by permission of the publishers.

From Rene Dubos, "We Can't Buy Our Way Out." Reprinted from *Psychology Today*, March 1970.

From F. Scott Fitzgerald, an excerpt reprinted by permission of Charles
Scribner's Sons from *The Great Gatsby*, pp. 1, 2, by F. Scott Fitzgerald. Copy-
right 1925 Charles Scribner's Sons; renewal copyright 1953 Frances Scott
Fitzgerald Lanahan. Adapted for the exercise by permission.

From Donald Fleming, "Big Science Under Fire." Reprinted from *The Atlantic*, September 1970.

From Félix Guirands, *Greek Mythology*, trans. Delano Ames. Adapted for
the exercise by permission of The Hamlyn Publishing Group Limited.

Preface

In this Fourth Edition the character of the *Practical English Handbook* has been refined but not changed. With the help of a teacher or independently, the college student needs a brief but practical guide to steer him as easily as possible through the intricate process of writing English prose. We hope to be that guide, to be efficient with the fewest possible words, to be helpful but never in the way.

Toward this aim we have made the book more concise where brevity can enhance clarity and more appealing to the eye where color can reinforce learning. For the student's further guidance, we have added a new section on writing about literature. The section on the investigative paper has been updated and a new model paper supplied. Users of previous editions of *PEH* will also notice throughout many new exercises, new specimen papers, and a continuing trend toward modernizing and simplifying.

These revisions of the handbook have been made after extensive consultation with teachers and scholars over the country who generously offered their constructive opinions. We have been especially indebted to Professor J. Carlton Nunan over the years and to Miss Ruth Walling.

Floyd C. Watkins
William B. Dillingham

Contents

Diction and Style *145*

The Process of Composition *184*

Writing and Revising

Whether the instructor uses this book as a basis for class discussions and exercises or for student self-help, it can be of great use in correcting and revising papers after he has marked and commented on them. The model paper on the following pages illustrates two ways in which an instructor may mark a paper for revision. It also shows the student author's corrections. In the left margin are section and subsection numbers. In the right margin are abbreviations asking for the same set of corrections. The instructor may prefer to use section numbers, abbreviations, or a combination of both methods. Sometimes he will write a comment that does not quite fit into either category.

The numerical symbols are given on the chart inside the front cover of this book. The abbreviations (with page numbers) are listed on the chart inside the back cover. With either method the student should study the relevant sections with their explanations, examples, and (if necessary) exercises, and make the appropriate corrections and revisions. These may range from removing an unnecessary comma to reorganizing and rewriting a paragraph or an entire paper.

The Trials of a Fast Eater
~~THE TRIALS OF A FAST EATER~~

no ital

Although he has not received much publicity, the fast eater

is a troubled and lonely person. When he goes out to dine with a

normal, or what is worse, a slow eater, he finishes first and in

agony sits there while his ~~dinning~~ dining partner continues to chew each   *sp*

mouthful ~~21~~ Twenty-one times. It is not possible to be comfortable under   *num*

such circumstances. ~~as these~~. He can try to make conversation,   *w*

but the slow eater may not want to talk. Talking interferes with

diligent chewing and slows one down even more. If the fast eater

just sits there and watches his companion finish‸ he feels like a   *pct*

~~peeping tom~~ Peeping Tom. The polite thing would seem to be to look away at   *cap*

the room and the customers‸ ~~however~~. However, the slow eater then tends to   *cs*

think that the fast eater is bored and in a hurry to leave, and

other people may think the fast eater is ~~starring~~ staring at them.   *sp*

Eating alone can be just as frustrating. Even if circum-

stances permit the fast eater to dine alone, there are drawbacks.

The first ~~being~~ is loneliness. But he faces problems greater than   *frag*

that. He may get the reputation of being anti-social. He feels

that people think he is alone because he does not like others or

because others do not like him. It is almost impossible to eat

alone‸ without being self-conscious and uncomfortable.   *pct*

A few fast eaters are ~~amune~~ immune to loneliness and can therefore   *sp*

dine alone. What happens when they have gulped down their

1

food? They wonder whether they should get up and leave or just
sit there at the table and try to look relaxed. Most fast eaters
choose to leave after they finish. When they do, they have that
feeling that people are saying, "He just got here; why is he
leaving?" "Is he sick?" "Is he angry because the food or service
is bad?" Or they may have the feeling that behind their back
people are whispering: "Shame, shame. He is so greedy; he bolts
his food like a savage."

There may appear to be an obvious answer to the plight of
the fast eater; simply ~~advice~~ advise him to become a slow eater. ~~It~~ Such a change
would improve not only his social image but his health as well.
Such advice is easy to give but nearly impossible to take. If
a person is told to breathe slower, he starts breathing faster.
He feels that he must get more oxygen. When one suggests to a
fast eater that he slow down, he speeds up. He is usually not
a ~~hog.~~ glutton. Something in his physical or psychological makeup drives
him to his deplorable condition. He will claim that he actually
enjoys his food more by getting it down as rapidly as possible.
The incurable fast eater should not lose hope, though. Modern
research is looking for a cure, and as long as men search for
answers, there is a chance. Meanwhile, he needs all the patience
and understanding that normal eaters can muster. He should not
be regarded as a gastronomical leper. After all, he is human, too.

Sentence Errors and Grammar

The most basic errors in sentences derive from sentence fragments (§ 1), from faulty connections between independent clauses (§ 2), and from changes in the forms of words (§§ 3–10).

1 Sentence Fragment *frag*

Do not use sentence fragments unless the alternatives are less effective.

A **fragment** is a part of a sentence written and punctuated as if it were a complete sentence. It may be a dependent clause, a phrase, or any other word group which violates the accepted subject-verb sentence pattern. Fragments usually reflect incomplete and sometimes confused thinking. In the following passage compare the fragments with the revisions.

FRAGMENTS

A student *leaving* home for the first time, *entering* college, *facing* many new responsibilities. (No verb—only three verbals.)

The arrangement of a schedule, the adjustment to new friends, the management of his budget. (No verb.)

No parents *calling* him several times before he gets out of bed each morning. (No independent clause.)

Teachers *who* merely make assignments without reminding the student to study. (Noun and "who" clause.)

That he should spend a certain amount of time on each unit of work. (Dependent clause.)

Because the freshman must become a man, live independently, and think for himself. (Dependent clause.)

COMPLETE SENTENCES

When a student *leaves* home for the first time and *enters* college, he *faces* many new responsibilities: (Now three verbs.)

↳ the arrangement of a schedule, the adjustment to new friends, the management of his budget. (Now series after colon.)

He cannot depend on his parents to call him several times before he gets out of bed each morning. (Subject and verb added.)

Teachers merely make assignments without reminding the student *to study.* ("Who" omitted.)

↳ and

↳ *to spend* a certain amount of time on each unit of work. (Parallel infinitives.)

The freshman must become a man, live independently, and think for himself. ("Because" omitted.)

Fragments are often used in conversation—and hence in written dialogue—when the meaning is clear from the context.

CONVERSATION "Have you ever voted?"
"Yes. Once. In the last election."

"See the geese."
"Where?"
"Flying north."

Sometimes in more formal kinds of writing, fragments create special effects or emphasis.

IN FICTION   He stood naked and alone in darkness, far from the lost world of the streets and faces; he stood upon the ramparts of his soul, before the lost land of himself; heard inland murmurs of lost seas, the far interior music of the horns. *The last voyage, the longest, the best.*

THOMAS WOLFE, *Look Homeward, Angel*

The fragment at the end of the following passage echoes the informality of speech.

IN EXPOSITION   It is one of the loveliest of stories. *So much irony; so much humour; so kind and understanding; and wrapped up in the most delicate poetic mood.*

SEAN O'FAOLAIN, *The Short Story*

This long fragment lacks subject and verb ("It has" or "It contains"), but the careful parallelism of the elements set off by semicolons indicates mastery—not ignorance or carelessness.

2 Comma Splices and Fused Sentences *cs/fus*

Use a semicolon or a comma and a coordinating conjunction (*and, but, or, nor, for, yet, so*) to join two independent clauses.

Use of a comma without a coordinating conjunction— **comma splice** or **comma fault**—suggests failure to recognize the line between independent clauses (or sentences).

Fused sentences occur when independent clauses (potential sentences) have neither punctuation nor coordinating conjunction between them. With no separation the clauses blur into each other.

Comma splices and fused sentences may be corrected in four principal ways:

(1) Use a *period* and write two sentences.
(2) Use a *semicolon*.
(3) Use a *comma* and a *coordinating conjunction*.
(4) Make one of the clauses *dependent*.

See also §23, The Colon.

SPLICE Human nature is seldom as simple as it appears, hasty judgments are therefore often wrong.

FUSED Human nature is seldom as simple as it appears hasty judgments are therefore often wrong.

CORRECTIONS
(1) Human nature is seldom as simple as it appears. Hasty judgments are therefore often wrong.
(2) Human nature is seldom as simple as it appears; hasty judgments are therefore often wrong.
(3) Human nature is seldom as simple as it appears, *and* hasty judgments are therefore often wrong.
(4) Because human nature is seldom as simple as it appears, hasty judgments are often wrong.

In any particular sentence, one solution may be more appropriate than others. Here (1), (2), and (4) seem preferable to (3) because "and" does not suggest the cause-effect relationship between "human nature" and "hasty judgments."

When possible, subordinate one clause or reduce it to a phrase or even a single word. In (4) one of the independent clauses is made a dependent adverbial clause. The sentence might also be rewritten as follows:

CLAUSE   Human nature is *so* complex *that hasty judgments are often wrong.*

or

PHRASE   Hasty judgments often overlook *the complexities of human nature.*

Before conjunctive adverbs (*however, moreover, therefore, furthermore,* etc.) use a semicolon to join independent clauses.

The rare book had a torn flyleaf; therefore it was advertised at a reduced price.

Exercise 1

Change the following fragments, comma splices, or fused sentences into correct sentences. Some sentences are already correct.

1. Unprincipled builders who seldom protect trees but often destroy, who move vast quantities of dirt but seldom plant.

2. Young people have always created their own varieties

of music. Growing older, they reject the music that comes after their youth.

3. In case of fire, one should never lose his head, on the contrary, he should think straight and act deliberately.

4. Most women seem to know more about men's clothing than men themselves do at any rate, they claim to know more.

5. Extreme nervousness sometimes makes a patient sullen and quiet. Then for no apparent reason arrogant and insulting.

6. New York's Washington Square has changed considerably since it was a haven for writers in the 1890's.

7. In a lonely village on the seacoast, where a man can still enjoy the primitive beauty of nature.

8. The Depression in the 1930's caused much unhappiness in some families, others it brought closer together.

9. Earth may be the only planet which will support human life. If man is to prosper, therefore, he must preserve his natural environment.

10. Man will sometimes participate in a pastime despite great danger, sky diving, for example, is perilous.

Exercise 2

Follow the instructions to Exercise 1.

1. After all, the students argued, any imbecile can punctuate, studying the mechanics of composition is a complete waste of time.

2. Most generous people are naive, they simply do not realize when they are being imposed upon.

3. The paranoid feels that the world is against him, consequently, he has no sense of guilt.

4. Some say that nonconformity has become a fad. Nonconformity for its own sake.

5. Several British novelists are also learned scientists or philosophers, C. P. Snow is a good example.

6. The art of pleasing is a very necessary one to possess. But a very difficult one to acquire.

7. Kindness can hardly be reduced to rules your own good sense and observation will teach you more about it than I can.

8. "Do as you would be done by" is the surest method I know of pleasing.

9. Observe carefully what pleases you in others, probably the same things in you will please others.

10. If you are pleased with the attention of others to your whims, your tastes, or your weakness. You can be sure that the same attention on your part will please them.

3 Verb Forms *vb*

Use the correct form of the verb.

All verbs have three principal parts: the present infinitive, the past tense, and the past participle. English verbs are regular or irregular in the formation of their principal parts.

Regular verbs (*help, talk, nail, open, close*) form the past tense and the past participle by adding *-d* or *-ed* or sometimes *-t* (as in *burnt, dwelt*). Thus the principal parts of the verb *to close* are *close, closed, closed;* those of *to talk* are *talk, talked, talked.*

Irregular verbs usually form the past tense and the past participle by a change in the root vowel: *drink, drank, drunk.* Consult a dictionary when in doubt; if only the infinitive form is given, the verb is regular. For an irregular verb like *think*, the dictionary also gives *thought* (the form of the past tense and the past participle) and *thinking* (the present participle). The principal parts are *think, thought, thought.* For a verb as irregular as *see*, the dictionary lists all three principal parts: *see, saw, seen.* You should know the principal parts of troublesome verbs so well that you automatically use them correctly.

Exercise 3

Cover the two right columns below and recite the principal parts of these verbs. Check any errors and study those you missed.

Principal Parts of Some Troublesome Verbs

INFINITIVE	PAST TENSE	PAST PARTICIPLE
awake	awoke, awaked	awoke, awaked
be	was	been
begin	began	begun

INFINITIVE	PAST TENSE	PAST PARTICIPLE
bid (to offer as a price or to make a bid in playing cards)	bid	bid
bid (to command, order)	bade, bid	bidden, bid
blow	blew	blown
burst	burst	burst
choose	chose	chosen
come	came	come
deal	dealt	dealt
dig	dug	dug
dive	dived, dove	dived
do	did	done
drag	dragged	dragged
draw	drew	drawn
drink	drank	drunk
drive	drove	driven
drown	drowned	drowned
fall	fell	fallen
fly	flew	flown
freeze	froze	frozen
give	gave	given
grow	grew	grown
hang (to execute)	hanged	hanged
hang (to suspend)	hung	hung
know	knew	known

INFINITIVE	PAST TENSE	PAST PARTICIPLE
lead	led	led
lend	lent	lent
ring	rang	rung
run	ran	run
see	saw	seen
shine (to give light)	shone	shone
shine (to polish)	shined	shined
shrink	shrank, shrunk	shrunk, shrunken
sing	sang	sung
sink	sank, sunk	sunk
swim	swam	swum
swing	swung	swung
take	took	taken
wear	wore	worn
write	wrote	written

In a few confusing pairs of verbs, it helps to remember that one is transitive (takes a direct object) and that the other is intransitive (does not take a direct object):

TRANSITIVE	lay (to place)	laid	laid
INTRANSITIVE	lie (to recline)	lay	lain
TRANSITIVE	set (place in position)	set	set
INTRANSITIVE	sit (be seated)	sat	sat
TRANSITIVE	raise (lift)	raised	raised
INTRANSITIVE	rise (get up)	rose	risen

Note that the intransitive verbs above have the root vowel *i* in the present tense form: *lie, sit, rise.*

Set also has intransitive forms: a hen *sets;* concrete *sets;* the sun *sets.*

Lie (to tell a falsehood) is intransitive like *lie* (to recline) but has different principal parts: *lie, lied, lied.*

4 Tense and Sequence of Tenses   *t/seq*

Use verbs carefully to express distinctions of time. Avoid unnecessary shifts in tense.

For each of the three divisions of time—present, past, and future—English verbs have three major tense forms: simple, progressive,[1] and perfect.

	IRREGULAR	REGULAR
SIMPLE		
Present	I go	I walk
Past	I went	I walked
Future	I shall (or will) go	I shall (or will) walk
PROGRESSIVE		
Present	I am going	I am walking
Past	I was going	I was walking
Future	I shall (or will) be going	I shall (or will) be walking
PERFECT		
Present	I have gone	I have walked
Past	I had gone	I had walked
Future	I shall (or will) have gone	I shall (or will) have walked

In general, the **present tense** expresses present time, but there are exceptions. Compare the following:

---

[1]Only the simple progressive forms are given here. There are in addition the forms with the auxiliary *do* (I *do read* regularly).

I *eat* lunch. (Simple present tense—with the force of repeated or habitual action.)

I *am eating* lunch. (Present progressive tense—present action.)

I *leave* for New York tomorrow. (Present tense—future action.)

I *am leaving* in fifteen minutes. (Present progressive tense—future action.)

As the last two examples illustrate, the time expressed by the tense form is often qualified or altered by an adverb or adverbial phrase.

Statements about the contents of literature and other works of art generally take the present tense (historical present).

In the novel *Little Big Man* General Custer madly **seeks** for power.

Statements of natural truth or scientific law take the present tense regardless of the controlling verb.

In 1851, Foucault proved that the earth *rotates* on its axis.

BUT Ancient Greek scholars *believed* that the earth *was* motionless.

The three **perfect tenses** are used in well-defined sequences. They indicate time or action completed before another time or action.

Use Present Perfect with Present:

I *have bought* my ticket, and I **am waiting** for the bus.

I *have* **already** *bought* my ticket. (Note that the controlling time word need not be a verb.)

Use Past Perfect with Past:
> I *had bought* my ticket, and I **was waiting** for the bus.
> I *had bought* my ticket before the bus **came**.

Use Future Perfect with Future:
> I *shall have eaten* by the time we **go**. (The controlling word, *go*, is present tense in form but future in meaning.)
> I *shall have eaten* by **one o'clock**.

The future perfect is rare. Usually the simple future tense is used with an adverb phrase or clause.

RARE   I shall have eaten before you go.

MORE COMMON I shall eat before you go.
       I shall eat before your departure.

In dialogue, the present tense is often used for the future or the future perfect.

> "When are you leaving?"
> "We leave at dawn." (*shall leave* or *shall have left*)

Relationships between verbs and expressions of time within statements should be logical and consistent:

TWO PAST ACTIONS
> The sailor *stood* on the shore and *threw* pebbles at the seagulls. (Not *throws*.)
> He *turned* away when he *saw* me watching him.

TWO PRESENT ACTIONS
> As the school year *draws* to a close, the students *are swept* into a whirl of activities.

FUTURE ACTIONS
> Some will go to the sea for their vacations, some will go to the desert, but few will go to the city.

An infinitive (see §49) generally takes the present tense

when it expresses action which occurs at the same time as that of the controlling verb.

I wanted *to go.*
NOT I wanted *to have gone.*

I had expected *to meet* my friends at the game.
NOT I had expected *to have met* my friends at the game.

I would have preferred *to wait* until they came.
NOT I would have preferred *to have waited* until they came.

The perfect participle (see §49) expresses an action which precedes another action.

Having completed the operation, the surgeon left at noon.

Exercise 4

Underline the incorrect verb and write the correct verb above it. Write C *at the left of correct sentences.*

1. Hundreds of unsold copies of the book which the author had recently published were laying on the shelves in his study.

2. The aged actor opened the Bible and begins reading the Song of Solomon.

3. It was Goethe's feeling that genius was simply "consummate industry."

4. Most alumni say that they would have preferred to have lived in dormitories.

5. When a man becomes a father, he keenly recognizes the new responsibilities that have been lain upon him.

6. After it sets, concrete is a durable material for roads.

7. Joseph Conrad was well into his thirties before he begun to write his novels.

8. After one has already bidden at an auction, it is too late for him to change his mind.

9. After the *Titanic* had sank, the world at first found the tragedy difficult to believe.

10. The Puritans were in some ways narrow-minded, but they lead lives of deep devotion to what they believed.

5 Voice *vo*

Use the active voice except when the context demands the passive.

A transitive verb is either active or passive. When the subject acts, the verb is active. When the subject is acted upon, the verb is passive. In most sentences the actor is more important than the receiver of the action. A weak passive verb makes a sentence flabby.

WEAK PASSIVE   The huge iceberg *was rammed* into by the luxury liner.
STRONG ACTIVE   The luxury liner *rammed* into the huge iceberg.
WEAK PASSIVE   A good race *was run* by the Ferrari.
STRONG ACTIVE   The Ferrari *ran* a good race.

The active voice helps to create a more concise and vigorous style, but the passive is useful for certain purposes:

(1) When the performer of an action is irrelevant or unimportant.

The book about motorcycles *had been misplaced* among books about cosmetics.

(2) When the emphasis is on the receiver, the verb, or even a modifier.

The police *were* totally *misled*.

6 Subjunctive Mood 𝓂𝓄

In using the subjunctive mood be guided by idiom.

The subjunctive in English has been traditionally employed to express commands, requests, wishes, and conditions which are improbable or contrary to fact. Today the subjunctive survives largely as a matter of idiom. In sentences like "I wouldn't do that if I *were* you," we are rarely aware of choosing the subjunctive. We are simply speaking idiomatically. Although we still say "I move that the meeting *be* adjourned," we are actually using a phrase which tradition has frozen into the language of parliamentary procedure. We do not usually say "If I *be*

right, that is a first edition." On occasion we may say "If
this be true"—but not often.

7 Subject and Verb: Agreement *agr*

**Use singular verbs with singular subjects, plural verbs with
plural subjects.**

The *-s* or *-es* ending of the third person present tense of
the *verb* is a sign of the **singular**; the *-s* or *-es* ending of a
noun is a sign of the **plural**.

SINGULAR   The dog barks. The ax cuts. The ax does cut.
PLURAL   The dogs bark. The axes cut. The axes do cut.

Most errors in agreement of subject and verb occur
with compound subjects or when a noun between subject
and verb is different in number from the subject.

7a A compound subject with *and* takes a plural verb.

Two or more subjects connected by a coordinating conjunction are said to be compound.

Work and *play* **are** not equally rewarding.

Baseball and *swimming* **are** usually summer sports.

EXCEPTION: Compound subjects connected by *and* but
expressing a singular idea take a singular verb.

A gentleman and a scholar **is** a man of manners and breadth.

When the children are in bed *the tumult and shouting* **dies.**

7b After a compound subject with *or, nor, either . . . or, neither . . . nor, not . . . but,* the verb agrees in number and person with the nearer part of the subject.

NUMBER Neither the *consumer* nor the *producer* is pleased by higher taxes.

Either *fans* or an *air conditioner* is necessary.

Either an *air conditioner* or *fans* **are** necessary.

PERSON Neither *you* nor your *successor* is affected by the new regulation.

Colloquially, a plural verb may be used to express a plural with *neither . . . nor.*

Neither *television* nor the *press* **are** unduly censored.

7c Intervening phrases or clauses not introduced by coordinating conjunctions do not affect the number of a verb.

The *engine* as well as the wings **was** destroyed in the crash.

The *pilot* along with all his passengers **was** rescued.

Connectives like *as well as* and *along with* are not coordinating conjunctions but prepositions; they do not form compound subjects. Other such phrases include *in addition to, together with, with,* and *including.*

7d A collective noun takes a singular verb when referring to a group as a unit, a plural verb when the members of a group are thought of individually.

A collective noun names a class or group: *family, flock,*

jury, congregation, etc. Meaning often determines number, but generally in American usage the collective noun is treated as singular.

> The *family* is going on vacation to Florida and the Caribbean. (Whether all together or some to Florida and some to the Caribbean.)

To avoid the unidiomatic "The family *are* going . . ." and to clarify the meaning, it would be better to recast the sentence.

> *Jean and I* are vacationing in Florida; the boys are going to the Caribbean.

7e Most nouns plural in form but singular in meaning take a singular verb.

Nouns such as *economics* and *news* are considered singular; others such as *trousers* and *scissors* are treated as plural except when used after *pair.* When in doubt, consult a dictionary. *Data* is considered singular or plural; the singular form, *datum,* is rare.

> *Economics* is often thought of as a science.

> The *news* of the defeat is disappointing.

> *Tactics* is the art of maneuvering military forces.

> British and American military *tactics* were different.

> The *data* about the rockets is confidential.

> The *trousers* are unpressed and frayed about the cuffs.

> An old *pair* of *trousers* is essential for the Bohemian.

The *scissors* **are** dull.

That *pair* of *scissors* **is** dull.

7f Indefinite pronouns such as *each, either, neither, one, no one, everyone, someone, anyone, nobody, everybody, somebody, anybody* usually take singular verbs.

Neither of his themes **was** acceptable.

Everybody **has** trouble choosing a subject for an essay.

Each student **has** chosen a subject for his report.

A plural verb with words like *each* is gaining some acceptance in colloquial English.

Each of the divers are allowed to follow their individual styles.

7g Some words, such as *none, some, part, all, half* (and other fractions), take a singular or a plural verb, depending on the meaning of the noun or pronoun which follows.

singular
Some of the *sugar* **was** spilled on the floor.

plural
Some of the *apples* **were** spilled on the floor.

singular
Half of the *money* **is** yours.

plural
Half of the *students* **are** looking out the window.

None is considered sometimes singular, sometimes plural:

None of those accused **was** really responsible.

None of those accused **were** really responsible.

"The number," when used as the subject, is usually singular:

The number of questions on the exam **was** twice as large as I expected.

"A number" is considered equivalent to the adjective *some*, and the following noun or pronoun controls the verb:

A number of the *guests* **were** whispering together.

7h In sentences beginning with *There* or *Here* followed by verb and subject, the verb will be singular or plural depending on the subject.

There and *Here* are devices (**expletives**) which let the subject follow the verb.

There **was** a long *interval* between the first and the second Crusades.

There **were** thirteen *blackbirds* perched on the fence.

Here **is** a *thing* to remember.

Here **are** two *things* to remember.

The singular *There is* may be used to introduce a compound subject when the first noun is singular.

There is a *swing* and a *footbridge* in the garden.

In sentences beginning with *It*, the verb is singular.

It **was** many years ago.

7i **A verb agrees with its subject, not with a subjective complement.**

Radio and *television* **are** his main source of pleasure.

His main *source* of pleasure **is** radio and television.

7j **After a relative pronoun (*who, which, that*) the verb has the same person and number as the antecedent.**

antecedent ⟶ *relative* ⟶ *verb of rela-*
         pronoun   *tive pronoun*

We   *who*   **are**   about to die salute you.

The *costumes which* **were** worn in the ballet were dazzling.

He was one *candidate who* **was** able to carry out his campaign pledges.

He was one of the *candidates who* **were** able to carry out their campaign pledges.

BUT   He was *the* only *one* of the candidates *who* **was** able to carry out his campaign pledges.

7k **A title is singular and requires a singular verb even if it contains plural words and plural ideas.**

The Canterbury Tales **is** a masterpiece of comedy.

"Prunes and Prisms" was a syndicated newspaper column on grammar and usage.

Exercise 5

Correct any verb which does not agree with its subject. If the sentence is correct, write C.

1. A large number of students are now moving away from housing provided by universities and colleges.

2. Suspended from the ceilings of the palace were a variety of chandeliers, some of sparkling crystal, others of gleaming brass.

3. Men in the "state of nature" were perpetually at war, and hence neither industry nor arts was possible.

4. D. H. Lawrence's *Sons and Lovers* are a landmark among the novels of its time.

5. At one time the North Star, one small point among the millions of heavenly bodies, were a guide to travelers in the northern hemisphere.

6. Ethics are the study of moral philosophy and standards of conduct.

7. Molasses were used in a great number of early New England recipes.

8. This tribal custom is enforced by strict taboos, the violation of which bring immediate death.

9. Childish sentences or dull writing are not improved by a sprinkling of dashes.

10. Neither money nor power are sufficient for a man who seeks to fulfill his greatest human potential.

Exercise 6

Correct any verb which does not agree with its subject.

For a certain kind of modern American, the two-weeks vacation have come to be looked upon as a panacea. All year long, the man who is shackled to his job look forward to the time when he can lounge in endless ease upon the shore of a mountain lake or the white sands of the sea. Sad to say, it is highly improbable that either the white sands or the mountain lake are the answer for this tense city-dweller. Anybody who live a life of quiet desperation for months or even years can hardly expect to forget anxieties at once. Nevertheless, realizing his extreme need to slow down, the American vacationer, along with his entire family, set out. Plan after plan have been made; nothing can go wrong. The trouble is that the family have made too many plans. Father is *determined* to relax. He somehow fails to see that relaxation and two weeks of feverish activity is not compatible. This man's situation, like that of thousands of others, are the result of his desire on the one hand to slow down and on the other to forget himself, to escape the thoughts that haunts him for fifty weeks of the year. To relax physically and at the same time to escape his frustrations are impossible for him. He thus returns to his job more weary or more worried or both than when he left. The roots of this man's problem goes very deep, and he must seek deep within himself for the solution. He must learn to stop frequently and to take account of himself and his values. He must identify himself with a standard of values which have been proved lasting. Above all, he must learn that there is much worse fates than falling behind the Joneses.

8 Pronouns: Agreement and Reference *agr/ref*

Use singular pronouns to refer to singular antecedents, plural pronouns to refer to plural antecedents.

A pronoun should clearly refer to a definite antecedent.

8a **In general, use a plural pronoun to refer to a compound antecedent with *and*.**

The *owner* and the *captain* refused to leave **their** distressed ship.

If two nouns designate the same person the pronoun of course is singular.

The *owner and captain* refused to leave **his** distressed ship.

8b After a compound antecedent with *or, nor, either . . . or, neither . . . nor, not only . . . but also*, a pronoun agrees with the nearer part of the antecedent. (See §7b.)

Neither the *Secretary* nor the *Undersecretary* was in **his** seat.

Neither the *Secretary* nor his *aides* were consistent in **their** policy.

A sentence like this written with *and* is less stilted.

The Secretary and his aides were not consistent in their policy.

Colloquially, a plural pronoun may be used to express a plural with *neither . . . nor*.

Neither *Nicholas* nor *Alexandra* lost **their** dignity under pressure.

8c A singular pronoun follows a collective noun antecedent when the members of the group are considered as a unit; a plural pronoun, when they are thought of individually. (See §7d.)

A UNIT   The student *committee* presented **its** report.

INDIVIDUALS   The *committee* filed into the room and took **their** seats, some of **them** defiant.

8d Such singular antecedents as *each, either, neither, one, no one, everyone, someone, anyone, nobody, everybody, somebody, anybody* usually call for singular pronouns.

Not *one* of the hunters felt that **he** had had a good day.

Everyone put **his** gun in the rack and went to his room to wash up for dinner.

NOTE: Use *his*, not the ungainly *his or her*, in a sentence like the following:

Each young rider took *his* (not *his or her*) horse successfully over the hurdles.

Use of a singular pronoun to refer to a singular antecedent is sometimes awkward.

Everybody cheered. I was pleased to hear him.

In colloquial speech like this, *to hear them* is acceptable.

8e *Which* refers to animals and things. *Who* refers to persons, but may be used with animals and some things called by name. *That* refers to animals or things and sometimes to persons.

The *boy* **who** was fishing is my son.

The *dog* **which** (or **that**) sat beside him looked listless.

Sometimes *that* and *who* are interchangeable.

A child *that (who)* sucks his thumb is often insecure.
A woman *that (who)* giggles is often insecure.
The man *that (who)* sold his business was financially insecure.

NOTE: *Whose* (the possessive form of *who*) is often used to avoid the awkward *of which*, even in referring to animals and things.

The *car* **whose** right front tire blew out crashed and burned.

8f Pronouns like *this, that, which,* and *it* should not vaguely refer to an entire sentence or clause.

CONFUSING   Some ballads hundreds of years old are still popular. *This* is one difference between them and modern country songs.

This could mean either that some ballads are still enjoyed or that they are hundreds of years old; or it may refer to the unexpressed idea that their age indicates an enduring quality which many modern country songs do not have.

CLEAR   Some ballads hundreds of years old are still popular. It is not likely that many modern country songs will have the same enduring value.

Many fuzzy references result from starting a sentence without foreseeing problems that will come up.

NOTE: In informal writing especially, experienced writers sometimes let *this, which,* or *it* refer to the whole idea of an earlier clause or phrase when no misunderstanding is likely.

The grumbler heard that his boss had called him incompetent. *This* made him resign.

8g Make a pronoun refer clearly to one antecedent, not uncertainly to two.

UNCERTAIN   Melville visited Hawthorne while he was American consul in Liverpool.

CLEAR   While Hawthorne was American consul in Liverpool, Melville visited him.

Exercise 7

Revise sentences that contain errors in reference of pronouns. Write C to the left of correct sentences.

1. This patient liked to play house when she was a child, but now in adulthood it does not appeal to her.

2. Battles between American Indians and white men came about in part because they oppressed them.

3. If one can be true to himself, you will never be false to others.

4. Some people claim that it is almost meaningless to send greeting cards, but others believe that it is worth preserving.

5. On the night of July 14, the patriots stormed the doors of the castle and the jails, and they were immediately smashed open.

6. Every physician will agree that his patient comes first unless he is unusually selfish.

7. Luck is a prerequisite to riches, which is why so few people are rich.

8. The poet is widely admired, but it is very difficult indeed to make a living at it.

9. The osprey feeds on fish, which it captures by diving into the water.

10. At present there are thousands of people trying to escape unemployment, yet they cannot find it in their cities.

Exercise 8

Revise sentences that contain errors in agreement of pronouns. Write C to the left of correct sentences.

1. The captain of the damaged plane let each member of the crew decide whether they wanted to remain with the ship or bail out.

2. On or before April 15, most American citizens file their income tax returns.

3. No matter what the detergent commercials say, no woman is really jubilant at the prospect of mopping their dirty kitchen floor.

4. The drifter, along with his many irresponsible relatives, never paid back a cent they borrowed.

5. Neither the batter nor the fans hesitated to show his ardent disapproval of the umpire's decision.

6. Everybody remembers the glamorous days of their childhood.

7. The League of Nations failed because they never received full support from the member countries.

8. Not every Victorian lady was as prudish as popular opinion would have them be.

9. Neither of the two old ladies ever admitted their guilt, but the police strongly suspected one of them of poisoning several magazine salesmen.

10. The group of several hundred students asked the president of the student body to speak to the dean on its behalf.

9 Case *C*

Use the correct case forms of pronouns. Learn when to use the possessive case forms of nouns.

To determine case, find how a word is used in its own clause — for example, whether it is a subject or a subjective complement, a possessive, or an object.

9a Use the subjective case for subjects and subjective complements.

SUBJECTS

This term *he and I* **have** not been inside the library. (Never *him and me.*)

It looked as if *he and I* **were** going to be blamed. (Never *him and me.*)

SUBJECTIVE COMPLEMENTS

The two guilty ones who went unpunished **were** *you and I.* (In formal usage, not *you and me.*)

It is I sounds punctiliously formal. In speech, *it's me* is almost universal. *It's us, it's him,* and *it's her* are common. In conversation *you and me* is sometimes used instead of *you and I* for the subjective complement.

9b Use the objective case for the object of a preposition.

FAULTY   The manager had to choose *between* **he and I.**

RIGHT   The manager had to choose *between* **him and me.**

Between is a preposition, and *him and me* is a compound object.

Be careful about the case of pronouns in constructions like the following:

FAULTY   A few *of* **we girls** learned how to cook.

RIGHT   A few *of* **us girls** learned how to cook.

When in doubt, test by dropping the noun: not *of we*, but *of us.*

9c Use the objective case for either the subject or the complement of an infinitive.

subject

The reporter considered **him** *to be* the best swimmer in the pool.

complement

The host finally discovered the uninvited guest *to be* **him.**

Normally such stilted constructions can be avoided by revising.

The host finally discovered that the uninvited guest was Sam.

9d **Put an appositive in the same case as the word it refers to.**

Pronoun appositives take different cases depending on the case of the word they refer to.

SUBJECTIVE Two *members* of the committee—**Bill** and **I**—were appointed by the chairman.

OBJECTIVE The chairman appointed two *members*—**Bill** and **me**.

9e **The case of a pronoun after *than* or *as* in an elliptical (incomplete) clause should be the same as if the clause were completely expressed.**

understood
↓
No one else in the play was as versatile as **she** *(was)*.

understood
↓
The director admired no one else as much as (*he admired* or *he did*) **her**.

9f **Use the possessive case for most pronouns preceding a gerund; a noun before a gerund may be possessive or objective.**

My *driving* does not overjoy my father.
The **soprano's** *singing* was not exactly fit for opera.

The noun is objective in certain instances:
(1) When a phrase intervenes:

There was a regulation against the **family** of a sailor *meeting* him at the dock.

(2) When a noun preceding the gerund is plural:

There is no rule against **men** *working* overtime.

(3) When a noun is abstract:

I object to **emotion** *overruling* judgment.

(4) When a noun denotes an inanimate object:

The crew did object to the **ship** *staying* in port.

When the verbal is a participle and not a gerund, the noun or pronoun preceding it is in the objective case.

I heard **him** *singing* loudly.
I hear **you** *calling* me.

9g Use an *of*-phrase to indicate the possessive with abstractions or inanimate objects.

INCONGRUOUS   The building's construction was delayed by lack of funds.

PREFERRED   The construction of the building was delayed by lack of funds.

There are well-established exceptions: e.g., *a stone's throw, for pity's sake, a month's rest, heart's desire, a day's work.*

9h The possessive forms of personal pronouns take no apostrophe; the possessive forms of indefinite pronouns require an apostrophe.

PERSONAL PRONOUNS   *yours, its, hers, his, ours, theirs*

INDEFINITE PRONOUNS   *everyone's, other's, nobody's, one's, anybody else's*

NOTE: Contractions such as *it's, he's, she's (it is, he is, she is)* require an apostrophe.

9i The case of an interrogative or a relative pronoun is determined by its use in its own clause.

Interrogative pronouns are *who, whose, whom, what, which* when used in questions. Relative pronouns are *who, whose, whom, what, which, that,* and the forms with *-ever,* such as *whoever* and *whosoever.* Those which give difficulty through change in form are *who* and *whoever. Who* and *whoever* are subjective; *whom* and *whomever* are objective.

The case of these pronouns is clear in uncomplicated sentences.

Who *defeated* Richard III?

But when something (usually a subordinate clause) intervenes between the pronoun and the rest of its clause, its function is sometimes obscured:

Who do the history books say *defeated* Richard III?

There are two simple ways of telling the case of the pronoun in such sentences:

(1) Mentally cancel the intervening words:

Who ~~do the history books say~~ defeated Richard III?

(2) Mentally rearrange the sentence in declarative order: subject – verb – complement:

The history books do say who defeated Richard III.

A similar procedure will work in determining that *whom* should be used.

At the beginning of a sentence in speech *who* is usually the form used for an object as well as for a subject:

Who were you talking *to* over there?

The case of a relative pronoun is determined by its use in its own clause, not by the case of its antecedent.

Here are three easy steps for checking this usage:

(1) Pick out the relative clause and draw a box around it.

This is the withered old man (**who, whom**) the artist said was his model.

(2) Cancel intervening expressions (*he says, it is reported,* etc.).

This is the withered old man (**who, whom**) ~~the artist said~~ was his model.

(3) Find the verb in the relative clause.

This is the withered old man **who whom** was his model.

subject   *verb*

NOTE: Do not confuse the function of the relative pronoun in its clause with the function of the clause as a whole.

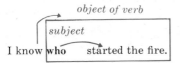

I know **who** started the fire.

object of verb

subject

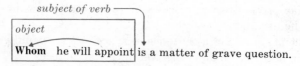

Try to avoid writing sentences with involved structure and elaborate clauses using *who* and *whom*.

Exercise 9

Underline the correct form in each of the following sentences.

1. No one knows the penalty for cheating more than (he, him).
2. On the platform stood the woman (who, whom) they all believed had practiced witchcraft.
3. On the platform stood the woman (who, whom) they all accused of practicing witchcraft.
4. The speaker defended his right to talk critically of (whoever, whomever) he pleased.
5. He (who, whom) would be great of soul must first know poverty and suffering.
6. Wise spending is essential to (us, we) poor music teachers.
7. On skid row is a little mission which gives (whoever, whomever) comes a hot meal, a dry place to sleep, and a word of encouragement.
8. Will the delegate from the Virgin Islands please indicate (who, whom) he wants to support?
9. It was (him, he) who discovered the buried cities of the Aztecs.
10. Truth is there for (whoever, whomever) will seek it.

Exercise 10

Underline the incorrect forms of pronouns and nouns, and write in the correct forms.

1. It was a good days work to repair the house's roof.

2. Women have motives and secrets that us men can never

   fathom.

3. Who's theory was it that matter can be neither created

   nor destroyed?

4. Its true the Potomac got it's name from the Indians.

5. I apologized because I wanted no ill feelings between

   he and I.

10 Adjectives and Adverbs *adj/adv*

Use adjectives to modify nouns and pronouns. Use adverbs to modify verbs, adjectives, and other adverbs.

Most adverbs end in *-ly*, whereas only a few adjectives (*lovely, holy, manly, friendly*) have this ending. Some adverbs have two forms, one with *-ly* and one without: *slow* and *slowly, loud* and *loudly*. Most adverbs are formed by adding *-ly* to adjectives: *warm, warmly; pretty, prettily*.

Choosing the correct adjective and adverb forms in sentences like the following is usually no problem.

> They stood *close*.
> The barber gave him a *close* shave.
> Study the text *closely*.

Use an adverb, not an adjective, to modify a verb, an adjective, or another adverb. Distinguish between *sure* and *surely*, *easy* and *easily*, *good* and *well*, *real* and *really*, *some* and *somewhat*, etc.

NOT   A *real* **good** high jumper *soars* over the bar **easy**.

BUT   A *really* **good** high jumper *soars* over the bar **easily**.

10a **Form the comparative and superlative degrees of most short adjectives and some adverbs by adding -*er* and -*est*. Use *more* and *most* (or *less* and *least*) before long adjectives, participles, and most adverbs.**

		COMPARATIVE	SUPERLATIVE
ADJECTIVES	dear	dearer	dearest
	pretty	prettier	prettiest
	but pitiful	more pitiful	most pitiful
	grasping	more grasping	most grasping
ADVERBS	slow	slower	slowest
	but rapidly	more rapidly	most rapidly

Certain adjectives and adverbs have irregular comparative and superlative forms: *good, better, best; well, better, best; little, less, least; bad, worse, worst;* etc.

Strictly speaking, some adjectives and adverbs are absolute; that is, they cannot be compared: e.g., *dead, perfect, complete, unique*. A thing cannot, logically, be more or less dead, or perfect, or unique (one of a kind). In formal writing use *more nearly perfect*, etc.

10b Use the comparative to refer to two things; the superlative, to more than two.

Both cars are fast, but the small car is (the) faster.
All *three* cars are fast. but the small car is (the) fastest.

10c Use a predicate adjective, not an adverb, after a linking verb such as *be, seem, become, look, appear, feel, sound, smell, taste.*

A predicate adjective describes the subject; an adverb modifies the verb.

He feels **bad**. (He is ill or depressed. *Feels* is a linking verb; it names a condition, not an action.)

He *reads* **badly**. (*Reads* expresses an action; it is not a linking verb.)

The *tea* tasted **sweet**. (*Sweet* describes the tea, not the manner of tasting.)

She *tasted* the tea **daintily**.

She *sang* **sweetly**. (*Sweetly* tells how she sang.)

10d Use an adjective, not an adverb, to follow a verb and its object when the modifier refers to the object, not to the verb.

Verbs like *keep, build, hold, dig, make, think* can link a subject and a subjective complement, as does the verb *to be*. Determine carefully whether to use an adjective or an adverb after verbs of this kind.

Keep your *clothes* **neat.** (Adjective — modifies complement.)

Keep your clothes **neatly** in the closet. (Adverb — modifies verb.)

Make my *bed* **soft.**

Make the bed **carefully.**

Exercise 11

Underline unacceptable forms of adjectives and adverbs and write the correct form. If a sentence is correct, write C.

1. Socrates thought deep about the nature and purpose of man.

2. Even though one may feel bad about his past acts, he can never change them.

3. The colonel would become real angry when anyone spoke against Kentucky.

4. It sure cannot be denied that Tennyson was one of the popularest poets of his time.

5. The ambassador spoke so rapid that no one interpreted him accurate.

6. The computer, a real complicated mechanical mind, is the most unique instrument of modern civilization.

7. The golfer's score was only average, but since he had often done so poorly, he felt good about it.

8. In the World Series, which league has won the most games?

9. In times of tribulation, you must think clear.

10. The manager, a man of indecision, never knew which of two possibilities was the best.

Sentence Structure

Sentences in good writing are varied in length, structure, and emphasis. Coordination, subordination, parallelism, and word order show relationships precisely and emphasize important elements of thought. The sections below discuss various structural problems and suggest devices for improving sentences in interest, force, and clarity.

11 Excessive Coordination ∞

Do not string together a number of short independent clauses.

Short independent clauses connected by coordinating conjunctions (*and, and so, but, or, nor, for, yet, so*) are wordy and monotonous. Excessive coordination fails to show precise relationships between thoughts. English is rich in subordinating connectives, and skillful writers know how to use them.

STRINGY   This mountain is six thousand feet high, *and* it is only four miles from the airport, *and* the field is not a very large one, *but* no plane has ever crashed on it.

If the final clause is most important, make it the only independent clause in a complex sentence retaining one *and*.

IMPROVED   *Although* this mountain is six thousand feet high *and* only four miles from the small airport, no plane has ever crashed on it.

STRINGY   The Senator was a liberal, *and so* he was in favor of the welfare program, *and* the new tax bill seemed to him inadequate, *and so* he voted against it.

IMPROVED   Being a liberal and feeling that the new tax bill was inadequate to support the welfare program, the Senator voted against it. (The first two clauses above have been subordinated and shortened; the participles, *being* and *feeling*, modify *Senator*.)

Exercise 1

Eliminate excessive coordination in the following by subordinating some of the ideas.

1. Women have been discriminated against, and they have been patient, but now they are complaining, and their cause is just.

2. Benjamin Franklin was an American, but he was at

home wherever he went, and so he gained wide popularity in France, and he was also well known in England.

3. The manta ray has a wide, flat body, and it is a member of the same class of fish as the shark.

4. Headhunters still exist in remote areas of the world, but they are rapidly disappearing, and today we seldom hear of them.

5. Computers calculate rapidly, and they do more work than man in the same time, and they threaten many jobs, but we must use them.

12 Subordination *sub*

Use subordinate clauses accurately and effectively.

Subordinate not only to avoid excessive coordination but also to achieve variety and emphasis. Insufficient or excessive subordination may ruin style. Selection of the proper thought to subordinate reveals the relative importance of ideas in a sentence.

12a Express main ideas in independent clauses, less important ideas in subordinate clauses.

An optimistic sociologist, who might wish to stress progress despite crime, would write:

> Although the crime rate is very high, man has progressed in many ways.

A pessimistic sociologist might wish the opposite emphasis:

> Although man has progressed in many ways, the crime rate is very high.

12b Avoid excessive overlapping subordinate constructions.

Monotony and even confusion can result from a series of clauses with each depending on the previous one.

OVERLAPPING   A watch is an intricate mechanism

which measures time,

which many people regard as the commodity

that is most precious.

IMPROVED   A watch is an intricate mechanism made to measure time, which many people regard as the most precious commodity.

Exercise 2

The following is an exercise in thinking and relationships, designed to point up differences in meaning that result from subordination. Read the pairs of sentences carefully and answer the questions.

1. A. After the Roman Empire was considerably weakened, corruption in high places became widespread.

   B. After corruption in high places became widespread, the Roman Empire was considerably weakened.

   Which of these sentences would a historian writing on the causes of Rome's fall be more likely to write?

2. A. Although a lifetime is short, much can be accomplished.

   B. Although much can be accomplished, a lifetime is short.

   Which of these sentences expresses more determination?

3. A. When in doubt, most drivers apply the brakes.

   B. When most drivers apply the brakes, they are in doubt.

   With which drivers would you prefer to ride?

4. A. In spite of the fact that he had a speech defect, Cotton Mather became a great preacher.

   B. In spite of the fact that he became a great preacher, Cotton Mather had a speech defect.

   In which sentence did he apparently overcome the defect?
   In which sentence did the defect remain noticeable?

5. A. While taking a bath Archimedes formulated one of the most important principles in physics.

   B. While formulating one of the most important principles in physics, Archimedes took a bath.

   Which sentence indicates accidental discovery?
   In which sentence does Archimedes take a bath for relaxation?

Exercise 3

Rewrite the following paragraph; avoid excessive overlapping subordination.

It is not possible to make the very best cheese in vast quantities at a low average cost because "scientific sampling" got in its statistically nasty work, which found that the largest number of people will buy something that is bland and rather tasteless. Those who prefer a product of a pronounced and individualistic flavor have a variety of preferences, although nobody is altogether pleased by bland foodstuff, in other words; even though nobody is very violently put off with the result that a "reason" has

been found for turning out zillions of packages of something that will "do" for nearly all and isn't even imagined
to be superlatively good by a single soul!

ADAPTED FROM PHILIP WYLIE, "Science Has Spoiled My Supper"

13 Completeness *inc*

Make your sentences complete in structure.

Sentences should be clear, and every element should be
expressed or implied clearly enough so that there is no
misunderstanding. Do not leave comparisons incomplete
and vague; do not omit necessary verbs, conjunctions, and
prepositions.

13a Make constructions with *so*, *such*, and *too* complete.

When there is a danger of misunderstanding, be sure that
the idea is expressed completely.

NOT CLEAR   The boy was too short. (Too short for what?)
            Those coins were so rare. (So rare that what?)

CLEAR   The boy was too short to play center.
            Those coins were so rare that even an expert could not
            identify them.

But to spell out all the implications of *so*, *such*, and *too* is
often unnecessary and pedantic.

CLEAR The boy didn't play center because he was too short.
I didn't go. I felt too sick.
Such nonsense!
We stayed indoors because it was such a miserable day.

13b Do not omit a verb or a preposition which the meaning of the sentence calls for.

Idiom sometimes demands a different form.

NOT He was simultaneously *repelled* and *drawn* **toward** the city.

BUT He was simultaneously *repelled* **by** and *drawn* **toward** the city.

BETTER He was simultaneously *repelled* **by** the city and *drawn* **toward** it.

OR He was simultaneously *repelled* and *attracted* **by** the city.

NOT In the confusion the *silver coins* **were** scattered and the *paper money* stolen. (Paper money *were* stolen?)

BUT In the confusion the *silver coins* **were** scattered, and the *paper money* **was** stolen.

However, when the same form is called for in both elements, it need not be repeated:

To err is human; to forgive, divine.

13c Omission of *that* sometimes obscures meaning.

OBSCURE The systems analyst found a worker who can increase his efficiency in this way does not tire.

CLEAR   The systems analyst found *that* a worker who can increase his efficiency in this way does not tire.

14 Comparisons *comp*

Make comparisons logical and clear.

Compare only similar terms.

The *laughter* of a loon is more frightening than an **owl**.

This sentence compares a sound and a bird. A consistent sentence would compare sound and sound or bird and bird.

The *laughter* of a loon is more frightening than the **hoot** of an owl.

A *loon* is more frightening than an **owl**.

The word *other* is often needed in a comparison:

ILLOGICAL   The Sahara is larger than any desert in the world.
RIGHT   The Sahara is larger than any *other* desert in the world.

Avoid awkward and incomplete comparisons.

AWKWARD AND   The lily is *as white* if not whiter **than** any other
INCOMPLETE   flower. (*As white* requires *as*, not *than*.)

BETTER   The lily is *as* white **as** any other flower, if not whiter.
              (*Than any other* is understood.)

AWKWARD AND   Yellowstone National Park is one of the most beau-
INCOMPLETE   tiful if not the most beautiful park in the United
              States. (After *one of the most beautiful*, the plural
              parks is required.)

BETTER	Yellowstone National Park is one of the most beautiful parks in the United States, if not the most beautiful.
OR	Yellowstone is one of the most beautiful national parks in the United States.
AMBIGUOUS	After many years my teacher remembered me better than my roommate. (Better than he remembered my roommate, or better than my roommate remembered me?)
CLEAR	After many years my teacher remembered me better than my roommate did.
OR	After many years my teacher remembered me better than he did my roommate.
FEEBLE	*Catch-22* is different.
CLEAR	*Catch-22* is different from other war novels of its time.

Exercise 4

Correct any errors in completeness and comparisons. Write C at the left of correct sentences.

1. The Moscow subway has for a long time and still is associated with the idea of progress for the Russian people.

2. When Alexander the Great was young he swore to hate Rome more than any man.

3. Visitors to New Lawson discover that the summers

there are as hot if not hotter than any they have ever experienced.

4. People go to Florida every winter because they feel that the winter climate is better than any state.

5. William always saw much more of his mother than his brother Henry.

6. Dr. Welby has and still does represent the dedicated family physician.

7. For one's health, plain water is as good if not better than most liquids.

8. The lighthouse stood as a symbol and guide to safety.

9. Some parents are so lax that they allow their children almost unlimited freedom.

10. Everything considered, the college years are usually more stimulating than the monotony and the bitter competition of making a living.

15 Consistency *cons*

Write sentences which maintain grammatical consistency.

Unnecessary changes in tense, person, mood, voice, relative pronoun, and kind of discourse are misleading and annoying.

15a Avoid unnecessary shifts between past and present tense.

Shifts in tense most frequently occur in narration.

NEEDLESS SHIFT FROM PAST TO PRESENT

The first night we *camped* by a stream, where dampness *entered* our very bones. Our joints *ached* when morning *came*, and we *decided* to move our tent. We *left* after breakfast, *spent* half the day looking for a better spot. Then I **find** an ideal place among a grove of trees. We **get** everything in place, **cut** back some bushes to make a larger clearing, and then we **see** it: NO TRESPASSING.

In writing about literature avoid shifting between past tense and the historical present.

NEEDLESS SHIFT FROM PRESENT TO PAST

Jane Austen's Emma *is* full of well-meant schemes for arranging other people's lives. She **persuaded** her little friend Harriet that Farmer Martin *is* not a socially acceptable suitor, and she *diverts* Harriet's affections to the Reverend Mr. Elton. When that plan **misfired**, she *is* ready with still another, which *ends* even more disastrously. From this and other experiences Emma **learned** that it **was** dangerous to meddle with the affairs of others, and she **was** honest enough to admit her faults. Harriet **was** at last united with the young farmer, and Emma *marries* the man who **had been** her unsparing critic.

Needless shifts between conditional forms (*should, would, could*) and other verb forms should also be avoided.

NOT Exhaustion after a vacation *could be* avoided if a family **can** plan better. (Use either sequence, *could . . . would,* or *can . . . can.*)

15b Avoid careless shifts in person.

In felling a tree, *a good woodsman* (**3rd person**) first cuts a deep notch near the bottom of the trunk and on the side toward which *he* (**3rd person**) wishes the tree to fall. Then *you* (**2nd person**) saw on the other side, directly opposite the notch. (The second sentence should read *Then he saws . . . .* Or the first, *you first cut . . . toward which you wish . . . .*)

15c Avoid unnecessary shifts in mood.

subjunctive
↓
SHIFTS It is necessary that the applicant *fill* in this form and
indicative
↓
mails it.

CONSISTENT SUBJUNCTIVE

It is necessary that the applicant *fill* in this form and *mail* it.

imperative   *indicative*
↓   ↓
SHIFTS First *mail* the application; then the applicant *will go* for an interview.

CONSISTENT IMPERATIVE

First *mail* the application; then *go* for an interview.

15d Avoid unnecessary shifts in voice.

POOR   The chef *cooks* (**active**) the shrimp casserole for thirty minutes and then it *is allowed* (**passive**) to cool.

BETTER   The chef *cooks* the shrimp casserole for thirty minutes and then *allows* it to cool.

15e Avoid unnecessary shifts from one relative pronoun to another.

SHIFT   She went to the cupboard *that* leaned perilously forward and *which* always resisted every attempt to open it.

CONSISTENT   She went to the cupboard *which* leaned perilously forward and *which* always resisted every attempt to open it. (Or, *that . . . that*.)

15f Avoid a shift from indirect to direct discourse in the same construction.

Indirect discourse paraphrases the speaker's words; direct discourse quotes exactly.

MIXED   ◄——————— *indirect* ———————►
The censor says that the book is obscene and
◄——————— *direct* ———————►
why would anyone wish to read it?

INDIRECT   The censor says that the book is obscene and asks why anyone would wish to read it.

DIRECT   The censor says, "The book is obscene. Why would anyone wish to read it?"

16 **Position of Modifiers** *po*

Place modifiers so that they clearly attach to the right word or element in the sentence.

A poorly placed modifier which floats loosely or attaches to the wrong word can cause confusion, misunderstanding, or unintended laughter. Usually a modifying adjective precedes its noun, whereas an adverb may precede or follow the word it modifies. Prepositional phrases usually follow closely, but may precede; adjective clauses follow closely; and adverbial phrases and clauses have a wide range of possible positions.

16a Avoid dangling modifiers.

Most danglers are verbal phrases at the beginning of a sentence, but there are many variations both in kind and in position.

DANGLING PARTICIPLE

Running along the street, my *nose* felt frozen. (A participle at the beginning of a sentence normally modifies the first noun or pronoun that follows. Here *running* seems to modify *nose*—as it could in a different context—and the proper agent, *I*, is not expressed.)

CLEAR

Running along the street, *I* felt as if my nose were frozen. (The participle here refers properly to *I*.)

OR

As I ran along the street, my nose *felt* frozen. (The participial phrase is now an adverbial clause, which modifies *felt*. *I* is expressed in the subordinate clause.)

DANGLING GERUND

After **snooping** around the attic, a *cowboy suit* was discovered. (The main clause is passive. Were it active, the gerund would attach to the proper agent—the person who did the snooping.)

CLEAR

After **snooping** around the attic, *I* discovered a cowboy suit. (Now all is well. Beware of the passive voice in such constructions.)

DANGLING INFINITIVE

To get well, an *operation* is necessary. (*To get well* refers to no word in this sentence.)

IMPROVED

To get well, *the patient* requires an operation.

DANGLING PREPOSITIONAL PHRASE

In old age, my father's *impatience* with new ideas became intolerable. (In whose old age? Impatience's? Of course not; my father's.)

CLEAR

In **his** old age, *my father's* impatience with new ideas became intolerable.

DANGLING ELLIPTICAL CLAUSE

While still sleepy and tired, the *counsellor* lectured me on breaking rules.

CLEAR

While I was still sleepy and tired, the counsellor lectured me on breaking rules.

Loosely attaching a verbal phrase to the end of a sentence is ineffective:

WEAK Students in a cooperative program may work part of the time thereby earning enough for all their expenses.

Often simple coordination is a good way to revise a sentence of this kind.

BETTER   Students in a cooperative program may work part of the time and earn enough for all their expenses.

Note that some verbal phrases need not refer to a single word in the sentence.

Strictly speaking, does this sentence contain a dangling construction?

To tell the truth, it does not.

The phrases are sentence modifiers.

16b Avoid misplaced modifiers.

The placement of a modifier in a sentence affects meaning.

He enlisted after he married *again*.

He enlisted *again* after he married.

Almost any modifier which comes between an adjective clause and the word it modifies can cause awkwardness or misunderstanding:

Wordsworth addressed a passage to his friend Coleridge in *The Prelude*, who collaborated with him in writing *Lyrical Ballads*.

Alchemy was the "science" of *transmuting lead into gold*, which was a common practice in the Middle Ages.

The first sentence is awkward though its intent is clear; the second is actually misleading.

In *The Prelude* Wordsworth addressed a passage to his friend Coleridge, who collaborated with him in writing *Lyrical Ballads*.

Alchemy, which was a common practice in the Middle Ages, was the "science" of transmuting lead into gold.

16c A modifier placed between two words so that it seems capable of modifying either is said to "squint."

UNCLEAR   The horse which was pawing *violently* kicked its owner.

CLEAR   The horse which was *violently pawing* kicked its owner.

OR   The horse which was pawing *kicked* its owner *violently*.

Exercise 5

Correct the faulty modifiers in the following sentences.

1. Dangling by one leg from a pair of tweezers, the little girl held the huge moth far out in front of her.

2. The courageous patient was able to walk about two weeks after the accident.

3. This computer is seldom used even though it is most effective because of the high cost.

4. To be absolutely certain, the answer must be checked.

5. Manufacturers are trying to develop a cigarette for smokers made of lettuce.

6. Serve one of the melons for dessert at lunch; keep one of them for the picnic in the refrigerator.

7. The carpenter inspected the board before sawing for nails.

8. At the age of five my grandfather told me about his life as a soldier.

9. Having been found guilty of drunken driving, the judge sentenced the young man to ninety days in jail.

10. The man who was writing hastily rose from the desk and left the room.

17 Separation of Elements *sep*

Do not unnecessarily separate closely related elements.

Separation of subject and verb, parts of a verb phrase, verb and object can be awkward or misleading.

AWKWARD The architect was, *having planned to go to Europe after finishing his degree and before he began his career*, disappointed not to receive a grant for foreign study.

IMPROVED *Having planned to go to Europe after finishing his degree and before he began his career*, the architect was disappointed not to receive a grant for foreign study.

AWKWARD Wild dogs had, *for several sleet-ridden and storm-ravaged winter days when food was scarce and the marrow seemed to freeze in the bones*, been seen on the hills.

IMPROVED *For several sleet-ridden and storm-ravaged winter days when the marrow seemed to freeze in the bones and food was scarce*, wild dogs had been seen on the hills.

LUDICROUS She is the man who owns the service station's wife.

ACCURATE She is the wife of the man who owns the service station.

Separation by short modifiers and phrases is often acceptable when it does not cause confusion. An adverb frequently precedes or follows a verb or comes between an auxiliary and a main verb:

The Cabots speak *only* to God.
It is *generally* known that bears love honey.

An adverb seldom comes between a verb and its object:

NOT John loves *exceedingly* Mary.
NOT John loves *better than anybody else in the whole world* Mary.

In such situations the adverb is best before the verb or after the object.

John loves Mary *exceedingly*.
John *never* loved Mary.
John loves Mary *better than he does anybody else in the world*.

In a sentence with both indirect and direct objects, the adverb tends to precede the verb; a modifier placed at the end of the sentence seems too far away.

> Joe *stealthily* handed me the petition.

It is usually best to avoid a **split infinitive** — one in which a modifier occurs between *to* and the verb form, as in *to loudly complain*. If any other position for the modifier is natural and clear, it is wise to put it there. Only occasionally is it less awkward to split an infinitive than not.

UNNECESSARY He felt it to *really* be impossible.

IMPROVED He felt it to be really impossible.

JUSTIFIABLE It would be wise for the student to clearly define his reasons for entering college.

In the last sentence above, the adverb would be awkward in any other position.

Do not divide a sentence with a quotation long enough to cause excessive separation.

AVOID Stephen Crane's view of the place of man in the world,

> A man said to the universe:
> "Sir, I exist!"
> "However," replied the universe,
> "The fact has not created in me
> A sense of obligation,"

is pessimistic.

18 Parallelism //

Use parallel grammatical forms to express elements parallel in thought. Constructions should be parallel in form if they are connected by coordinating conjunctions (*and, but,*

or, nor) or by correlative conjunctions (*either . . . or, neither . . . nor, not . . . but, not only . . . but also, both . . . and*).

Words go with similar words, phrases with similar phrases, clauses with similar clauses.

NOT PARALLEL   *All play* and *not working* makes a boy dull.
PARALLEL   *All play* and *no work* makes a boy dull.

NOT PARALLEL

Jason Compson advises his son $\begin{cases} \textit{to forget } \text{time} \\ \text{and} \\ \textit{against trying } \text{to conquer it.} \end{cases}$

PARALLEL

Jason Compson advises his son $\begin{cases} \textit{to forget } \text{time} \\ \text{and} \\ \textit{not to try } \text{to conquer it.} \end{cases}$

NOT PARALLEL

The collector promises $\begin{cases} \textit{to buy a copy } \text{of the rare book} \\ \text{and} \\ \textit{that the cost } \text{will not be excessive.} \end{cases}$

PARALLEL

The collector promises $\begin{cases} \textit{that he will buy } \text{a copy of the rare book} \\ \text{and} \\ \textit{that the cost will not be excessive.} \end{cases}$

AWKWARD CORRELATIVES

verb   *pronoun*
The reactionary *not only* supported tyranny *but also* he became a tyrant.

PARALLEL

verb   *verb*
The reactionary *not only* supported tyranny *but also* became a tyrant.

Exercise 6

Revise any sentences with faulty parallelism. Write C to the left of correct sentences.

1. The ideal piecrust is tender, flaky, and, of course, tastes good.

2. Have you considered buying one of those small foreign cars that are so economical and how easy they are to park?

3. Adjusting to a large college is very difficult for a person who has attended a small school all of his life and being used to more individual attention.

4. There is no better way to spend a summer than roaming through the great north woods, camping by a lake, and forgetting the cares of civilization.

5. To be a good listener one must have a genuine interest in people, a strong curiosity, and discipline oneself to keep the mind from wandering.

6. *Death of a Salesman* is a play about a man who wasted his life and which teaches the need of self-discovery.

7. A good criminal lawyer must be well educated in his profession and something of an actor.

8. The delegation found it impossible either to see the governor or even his secretary.

9. Most slow readers could read much faster and better if they would not glance back over lines they have passed and also moving their lips when they read.

10. The jaguar is swift, quiet, and moves with grace.

19 Variety in Sentences 𝓋𝑎𝓇

Vary your sentences in length, structure, and order.

Length An unbroken string of short sentences becomes monotonous and fails to indicate such relationships as cause, condition, concession, time sequence, and purpose.

CHOPPY Overpopulation is becoming a problem. Alaska is not thickly populated. Many people may move there. It has vast open lands.

Most passages like the one above contain excess fat—wordiness and repetition (see § 38). These sentences can be combined into a complex sentence which shows more exactly the relationships of the thoughts.

IMPROVED Alaska, a relatively unpopulous state, has vast open lands which may attract many people in this time of overpopulation.

Structure Do not overuse one kind of sentence structure. Write simple, compound, and complex patterns, and vary your sentences between loose, periodic, and balanced forms.

A **loose sentence,** the most frequent kind, makes its main point early and then adds refinements. In contrast, a **periodic sentence** withholds an element of the main thought until the end and thus creates suspense and emphasis.

LOOSE The real trouble about women is that they must always go on trying to adapt themselves to men's theories of of women as they always have done. D. H. LAWRENCE

LOOSE *Uncle Tom's Cabin* is a very bad novel, having, in its self-righteous, virtuous sentimentality, much in common with *Little Women*. JAMES BALDWIN

PERIODIC Under a government which imprisons any unjustly, the true place for a just man is also a prison.

HENRY DAVID THOREAU

PERIODIC There is one thing above all others that the scientist has a duty to teach to the public and to governments: it is the duty of heresy. J. BRONOWSKI

A **balanced sentence** has parts which are similar in structure and length and which express parallel thoughts. Indeed, balance is simply another word for refined and extended parallelism. (For a discussion of parallel structure see §18.) Notice the perfect symmetry in the following sentence: "Marriage has many pains, but celibacy has no pleasures" (SAMUEL JOHNSON).

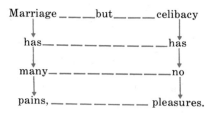

A sentence can also be balanced if only parts of it are symmetrical: "Thus the Puritan was made up of two different men, the one all self-abasement, penitence, gratitude, passion; the other proud, calm, inflexible, sagacious" (THOMAS BABINGTON MACAULAY).

> Thus
> the Puritan
> was made up
> of two different men,
>
> the one_ _ _ _ _ _the other
> all self-abasement, _ _ _ _ proud,
> penitence,_ _ _ _ _ _ calm,
> gratitude, _ _ _ _ inflexible,
> passion;_ _ _ _ _sagacious.

Order If all your sentences follow the normal order of subject-verb-complement, the effect can be monotonous. For interest and emphasis invert the order occasionally, and avoid invariably tacking all dependent clauses and long phrases on at the end. Study the variations in the following sentences.

NORMAL ORDER

subject   *verb*   *object*   *modifiers*

She attributed these *defects* in her son's character to the general weaknesses of mankind.

SENTENCE BEGINNING WITH DIRECT OBJECT

These *defects* in her son's character she attributed to the general weaknesses of mankind.

SENTENCE BEGINNING WITH PREPOSITIONAL PHRASE

To the general weaknesses of mankind she attributed the defects in her son's character.

SENTENCE BEGINNING WITH ADVERB

Slowly she rose to dance.

INVERTED SENTENCE BEGINNING WITH CLAUSE USED AS OBJECT

That the engineer tried to avert the catastrophe, none of them would deny.

INVERTED SENTENCE BEGINNING WITH DEPENDENT ADVERBIAL CLAUSE

If you wish to create a college, therefore, and are wise, you will seek to create a life.   WOODROW WILSON

SENTENCE BEGINNING WITH PARTICIPIAL PHRASE

Flying low over the water for hours, the plane searched for survivors.

In climactic order, the elements of a series are arranged in the order of increasing importance. The order of decreasing importance may result in anticlimax and loss of emphasis.

UNEMPHATIC   The hurricane left thousands of people homeless, ruined the crops, and interrupted transportation.

CLIMACTIC   The hurricane interrupted transportation, ruined the crops, and left thousands of people homeless.

Exercise 7

Make one sentence out of each of the groups below.

1. At the age of seventeen I went to debate at a high school.
   Three girls went with me.
   It was the fall of my senior year.
   The high school was over a hundred miles away.

   ADAPTED FROM JOHN UPDIKE

2. There is, indeed, much wrong with cities.
   Big ones and little ones have problems.
   They should not be abandoned.
   We should not rebuild them on abstract principles.

   ADAPTED FROM ROBERT MOSES

3. Philadelphia is one of America's most historic cities.
   At present it is involved in a program of urban renewal.
   This program is already showing substantial results.

4. Van Gogh was a French painter.
   He belonged to the Impressionist School.
   Van Gogh once cut off his ear with a razor.
   At that time he was in one of his frequent fits of de
   pression.

5. Some people think mountain climbing is silly.
   They do not really understand.
   A mountain climber is meeting a challenge.
   It is a symbolic challenge.
   The mountain represents the seemingly invincible ob-
   stacles of life.

Exercise 8

Rewrite the following sentences and make them periodic. If you consider a sentence already periodic, put a check mark by it.

1. One machine, the typewriter, revolutionized business practices and had a profound influence on the style of many authors.

2. A sense of humor is one quality no great leader can be without.

3. Selfishness, some philosophers maintain, is the reason behind every action of any person.

4. The blue whale is the largest known creature on earth.

5. He studied when all other possible methods of passing

the course proved unworkable.

Exercise 9

Rewrite the following sentences to give them balanced constructions. If a sentence already has a balanced construction, put a check mark by it.

1. The rewards of youth are obvious, but much more subtle are the rewards of age.

2. A successful advertisement surprises and pleases, but not all advertisements are successful because some are merely boring and irritating.

3. A realist knows his limitations; a romantic knows only what he wants.

4. The politician is concerned with successful elections whereas the future of his people is foremost in the mind of a statesman.

5. A trained ear hears many separate instruments in an orchestra, but the melody is usually all that is heard by the untutored.

Exercise 10

Rewrite the following sentences according to the principles of climactic order.

1. Our space ship brought back from the strange planet a large animal, two small green men, and a soil sample.

2. John Quincy Adams served in more than seven political offices; he was President of the United States, a Senator, and a Congressman.

3. Plagues in the Middle Ages were probably the greatest kind of national disaster; millions of people suffered death, great pain, and economic losses.

4. Cities are faced with countless problems such as crime in the streets, littering, pollution, and traffic jams.

5. Although the controversial speaker tried to proceed, he

was forced to stop because of a stone that struck him between the eyes, annoying catcalls, and a barrage of rotten fruit.

Exercise 11

Show how variety is achieved in the following paragraph.

The legend of the theft of Indian land has been a romantic myth. Eskimo leader William Hensley said of this vanishing land: "It was by the use of laws that our people have been deprived of their land." Most of their land was taken from them with unscrupulous legality by treaties ratified by the Congress and signed by the government. Treaties of peace they were called. But they were little more than real-estate deals. From 1778 to 1868, in ninety years, there were 370 of these treaties signed by the federal nation with the Indian nations. The Cherokees signed twenty-two. The Delawares signed twenty-five.

The Sioux signed thirty-nine. The Chippewas and the Potawatomi signed forty-seven each. There were so many treaties not because there so many Indian Wars, but because there were so many Indian lands that the tribes were forced, or enticed, to sign away.

STAN STEINER, *The New Indians*

Exercise 12

Rewrite the following passage so that it is more varied in sentence structure.

An Italian, Cristoforo Colombo, discovered America. Another, Amerigo Vespucci, gave it his name. Neither Italians as a people nor Italy as a country had a significant place in the early history of the United States. During the colonial period, a few men from the Italian peninsula settled in America. They lived in the cities along the Atlantic seaboard. This sprinkling of Italians left no noteworthy mark on the life of the English colonies. In 1621, a small group of Italian glassmakers lived in Jamestown. They made an impression. It was negative. According to the secretary of that colony, "a more damned crew hell never vomited."

The largest group of Italians to settle in North America consisted of about 200. They were Protestants. They had lived in the valleys of Piedmont. They were usually called "Waldensians" after Peter Waldo of Lyon. He was a merchant. He founded their sect. They suffered persecution and massacre at home. Then they fled to Holland. From there they sought refuge in the New World. They arrived in New Amsterdam in the spring of 1657. A few weeks after their arrival, they moved on to Delaware. There Dutch Protestants purchased land for them. The Italians organized the first government of New Amstel. Later it was called New Castle. Historians know little about these settlers and their movements. They do know they were Italians. They spoke and kept their records in French. They know too that a small band of them also established a settlement at Stony Brook, New York.

ADAPTED FROM ALEXANDER DECONDE, *Half Bitter, Half Sweet: An Excursion into Italian-American History*

Punctuation

Punctuation marks separate, group, and qualify words and elements in sentences; they help to suggest the pauses, intonations, and gestures that would be used in speech. Many choices are available to a writer in any substantial passage of writing, and they have effect on meaning.

20 The Comma ,

Use commas to reflect structure and to clarify the sense of the sentence.

The **comma** is chiefly used (1) to separate equal elements, such as independent clauses and items in a series, and (2) to set off modifiers or parenthetical words, phrases, and clauses. Elements which are set off within a sentence take a comma both *before* and *after*.

NOT   This novel, a best seller has no real literary merit.

BUT   This novel, a best seller, has no real literary merit.

20a Use a comma to separate independent clauses joined by a coordinating conjunction.

Nice is a word with many meanings, and some of them are opposite to others.

Sherlock Holmes had to be prepared, for Watson was full of questions.

NOTE: The comma is sometimes omitted when the clauses are short and there is no danger of misreading.

The weather was clear and the pilot landed.

20b Use a comma between words, phrases, or clauses in a series.

The closet contained worn clothes, old shoes, and dusty hats.

The final comma before *and* in a series is sometimes omitted.

The closet contained worn clothes, old shoes and dusty hats.

But the comma must be used when *and* is omitted.

The closet contained worn clothes, old shoes, dusty hats.

And it must be used when the final elements could be misread.

An old chest in the corner was filled with nails, hammers, a hacksaw and blades, and a brace and bit.

Series of phrases, of dependent clauses, or of independent clauses are also separated by commas.

PHRASES   We hunted for the letter in the album, in all the old trunks, and even under the rug.

DEPENDENT CLAUSES	Finally we guessed that the letter had been burned, that someone else had already discovered it, or that it had never been written.
INDEPENDENT CLAUSES	We left the attic, Father locked the door, and Mother suggested that we never unlock it again.

In a series of independent clauses, the comma is not omitted before the final element.

Exercise 1

Insert commas where necessary in the following sentences.

1. I knew that she was smiling at me but somehow I could not force myself to look in her direction again.
2. The long novels *Moby-Dick* and *War and Peace* take many hours to read but they reward one completely with their richness of meaning their fullness of character portrayal and their moments of intense excitement.
3. The hamper was filled with cold cuts mixed pickles bread and butter.
4. The hunter should go into the blind load his gun sit perfectly still and wait patiently.
5. Some government documents are classified secret for the safety of the country must be preserved.
6. The sensitive child knew that the earth was round but she thought that she was on the inside of it.

7. The instructor said that the class had not been doing very well that obviously everyone had failed to take notes and that he wanted to see some improvement.

8. For breakfast she served us bacon and eggs toast and jelly and hot coffee.

9. Careless driving includes speeding stopping suddenly making turns from the wrong lane of traffic going through red lights and so forth.

10. Driving was easy for a great part of the way was paved and traffic was light.

20c Use a comma between coordinate adjectives not joined by *and*. Do not use a comma between cumulative adjectives.

Coordinate adjectives modify the noun independently. Cumulative ones modify not only the noun, but the whole cluster of intervening adjectives.

Note the difference:

COORDINATE

Madame de Stael was an attractive, gracious lady.

Ferocious, vigilant, loyal dogs were essential to safety in the Middle Ages.

CUMULATIVE

The uninvited guest wore a dark blue tweed suit.

The witch turned out to be just a wizened little old woman.

Two tests are helpful.

Test One   *And* is natural only between coordinate adjectives.

> an attractive *and* gracious lady
> ferocious *and* vigilant *and* loyal dogs

But not—

> dark *and* blue *and* tweed suit
> wizened *and* little *and* old woman

Test Two   Coordinate adjectives are easily reversible.

> a gracious, attractive lady
> loyal, vigilant, ferocious dogs

But not—

> tweed blue dark suit
> old little wizened woman

The distinction is not always clear-cut, however, and the sense of the cluster must be the deciding factor.

She was wearing a full-skirted, low-cut velvet gown.

(A velvet gown that was full-skirted and low-cut; not a gown that was full-skirted and low-cut and velvet.)

Note that a comma is not used before the noun:

NOT	gracious, lady	BUT	gracious lady
	ferocious, dogs		ferocious dogs

Exercise 2

Punctuate the following. When in doubt apply the tests described above.

1. a graceful agile cat
2. large glass front doors
3. a little black recipe book
4. a high-crowned lemon-yellow felt hat
5. a wrinkled brown paper bag
6. a hot sultry depressing day
7. the gloomy forbidding night scene
8. straight strawberry-blond hair
9. a woebegone ghostly look
10. beautiful imported Persian rugs.

20d Use a comma after a long introductory subordinate phrase or clause.

LONG PHRASE With this bitter part of the ordeal behind him , the trapper felt more confident.

LONG CLAUSE When this bitter part of the ordeal was behind him , the trapper felt more confident.

When the introductory element is short and there is no danger of misreading, the comma is often omitted.

SHORT PHRASE After this bitter ordeal the trapper felt more confident.

SHORT CLAUSE When this ordeal was over the trapper felt more confident.

Commas after these introductory elements would not be definitely wrong. Use of the comma sometimes depends on personal taste.

Regardless of length, introductory participial, infinitive, and gerund phrases are usually set off by commas.

PARTICIPLE Living for centuries, redwoods often reach a height of three hundred feet.

INFINITIVE To verify or correct his hypothesis, a scientist performs an experiment.

GERUND After surviving this ordeal, the trapper felt relieved.

A phrase or a clause set off by a comma at the beginning of a sentence may not require a comma if it is moved to the end of the sentence.

BEGINNING When speaking of the difficult times of the past, the old are often nostalgic.

END The old are often nostalgic when speaking of the difficult times of the past.

20e Use commas to set off nonrestrictive appositives, phrases, and clauses. Do not use commas to set off restrictive appositives, phrases, and clauses.

A **restrictive modifier** points out or identifies its noun or pronoun; remove the modifier, and the sentence radically changes in meaning or becomes nonsense. A **nonrestrictive modifier** describes and adds information but does not point out or identify; omit the modifier, and the sentence loses some meaning but does not change radically or become meaningless.

RESTRICTIVE   Taxicabs *that are dirty* are illegal in some cities.

Water *which is murky in appearance* should always be boiled before drinking.

The play *Hamlet* has been a scholar's delight for over three hundred years.

In all these sentences, the italicized expressions identify the words they modify; to remove these modifiers is to change the meaning radically or to leave the sentence an empty shell. Contrast with the following:

NONRESTRICTIVE   Taxicabs, *which are always expensive,* cost less in New York than elsewhere.

Oil, *which is lighter than water,* rises to the surface.

Shakespeare's last play, *The Tempest,* is optimistic and even sunny in mood.

In these sentences the italicized modifiers add information, but they do not point out or identify. They do not tell which taxicabs, what kind of oil or water, and so on. They expand the meaning of the sentence, but are not essential to it.

NOTE: *That* never introduces a nonrestrictive clause.

Modifiers in some sentences can be either restrictive or nonrestrictive, and use or omission of the commas changes the sense.

The coin which gleamed in the sunlight was a Spanish doubloon. (There were several coins.)

The coin, which gleamed in the sunlight, was a Spanish doubloon. (Only one coin.)

In speech, a nonrestrictive modifier is usually preceded by a pause whereas a restrictive modifier is not.

Exercise 3

The following pairs of sentences illustrate differences in meaning that result from use of commas to set off modifiers. Answer the questions about each pair of sentences.

1. A. The hitchhiker leaning against the post seemed totally indifferent about getting a ride.
   B. The hitchhiker, leaning against the post, seemed totally indifferent about getting a ride.

   How many hitchhikers are there in sentence A? Sentence B?

2. A. The compulsory school law, which has just been passed, strongly insures educational training for all children.
   B. The compulsory school law which has just been passed strongly insures educational training for all children.

   Which sentence refers to a place which has never before had a compulsory school law?

3. A. Men often say that women drivers, who are not well trained, cause most of our minor automobile accidents.
   B. Men often say that women drivers who are not well trained cause most of our minor automobile accidents.

   Which sentence shows a greater prejudice against women drivers?

4. A. Anthropologists, who respect native ways, are welcome among most tribes.

B. Anthropologists who respect native ways are welcome among most tribes.

Which sentence reflects confidence in anthropologists?

5. A. The kitten which has a white ring around its tail is exceptionally frisky.
   B. The kitten, which has a white ring around its tail, is exceptionally frisky.

How many kittens is the speaker watching in sentence A? In sentence B?

Exercise 4

Insert needed commas for nonrestrictive modifiers; circle all unnecessary commas. Write C to the left of correct sentences.

1. The name Rover was often associated with dogs which were stupid and happy.

2. Barbers, who are bald, are frequently the ones who are most authoritative in discussing baldness with their customers, who are worrying about losing their hair.

3. The wealthy, who keep their expensive jewelry in bank vaults, sometimes hire people to wear their pearls for them so that the gems will not lose their luster.

4. Vests which were once very popular were out of vogue for several decades.

5. Adam's son Abel was a shepherd.

6. Abel Adam's son was a shepherd.

7. Across the bay lived Alan J. Allen the millionaire, and only three or four hundred yards away was the palatial home of Osgood England the soap king.

8. The brothers of Jacob's son Joseph sold him to some Midianites who in turn sold him into Egypt.

9. Sherwood Anderson's book, *Poor White,* is one of the author's strongest expressions of the recurrent theme, that industrialism caused human frustrations never felt before.

10. Tom and his wife Daisy had traveled over the world, moving from one place to another and finally settling down in a huge mansion in East Egg which is on Long Island.

20f Use commas with sentence modifiers, conjunctive adverbs, and sentence elements out of normal word order.

Sentence modifiers like *on the other hand, for example, in fact, in the first place, I believe, in his opinion, unfortunately,* and *certainly* are set off by commas.

> Only a few poets, unfortunately, make a living by writing.
> Wells's early novels, I believe, stand the test of time.

Commas are frequently used with conjunctive adverbs, such as *therefore, moreover, then, consequently, nevertheless.*

optional

BEFORE CLAUSE The secretary checked the figures once more; therefore, the mistake was discovered.

WITHIN CLAUSE The secretary checked the figures once more; the mis-

optional

take, therefore, was discovered.

Commas always set off *however* used as a conjunctive adverb.

The auditor found the error in the figures; however, the books still did not balance.

The auditor found the error in the figures; the books, however, still did not balance.

Commas are not used to set off *however* as an adverb meaning "no matter how."

However fast the hare ran, he could not catch the tortoise.

Use commas if necessary for clearness or emphasis when part of a sentence is out of normal order.

Aged and infirm, the President governed through his loyal ministers.

OR The President, aged and infirm, governed through his loyal ministers.

BUT The aged and infirm President governed through his loyal ministers.

20g Use commas with degrees and titles and elements in dates, places, and addresses.

DEGREES AND TITLES

William Snipes, M. A., came to the reception.

Charles Morton, Jr., Chairman of the Board, departed.

DATES

Sunday, May 31, is . . . .

August 1973 was . . . OR August, 1973, was . . . . (Either is acceptable.)

December 31, 1970, was . . . . (Use commas *before* and *after*.)

. . . 31 December 1970 was . . . . (No commas required.)

The year 1968 was . . . . (Restrictive; no commas.)

PLACES

Cairo, Illinois, is . . . . (Use commas *before* and *after*.)

ADDRESSES

Write the editor of *The Atlantic*, 8 Arlington Street, Boston, Massachusetts 02116.

20h Use commas for contrast or emphasis and with short interrogative elements.

The pilot had been forced to use an auxiliary landing field, not the city airport.

The field was safe enough, wasn't it?

20i Use commas with mild interjections and words like *yes* and *no*.

Well, I did not think it was possible.
No, it proved to be quite simple.

20j Use commas with words in direct address and after the salutation of a personal letter.

Mary, have you seen the portrait?

Dear John,
    It has been some time since I've written . . . .

20k Use commas with expressions like *he said*, *he remarked*, and *he replied* when used with quoted matter.

"I am planning to give up Latin," she remarked, "at the beginning of next term."

He replied, "It's all Greek to me."

20L Set off an absolute phrase with commas.

An **absolute phrase** consists of a noun followed by a modifier. It modifies the sentence as a whole, not any single element in it.

absolute phrase
Our journey over, we made camp for the night.

←—— *absolute phrase* ——→
The portrait having dried, the artist hung it on the wall.

20m Use commas to prevent misreading or to mark an omission.

After washing and grooming, the pup looked like a new dog.
When violently angry, elephants trumpet.
Beyond, the open fields sloped gently to the sea.

is omitted
↓
To err is human; to forgive, divine.

Exercise 5

*Add necessary commas. If a sentence is correct as it
stands, label it* C.

1. Inside the convention hall resembled a huge over-
   crowded barn.

2. A short time before he departed he bowed to his host-
   ess who returned his mock courtesy and said softly
   "Thank you."

3. Seeing a nightingale he recognized its resemblance to
   other members of the thrush family.

4. Despite the old saying to the contrary you can sometimes tell a book by its cover.

5. The Vandyke beard according to authorities was
   named after Sir Anthony Van Dyck a famous Flemish
   painter.

6. An old newspaper dated December 31 1900 was still
   behind the paneling and the antique dealer carefully
   removed it.

7. Only after reading a book either very carefully or
   more than once should a critic write a review.

8. While burning cedar has a distinct and strong odor.

9. The cloverleaf a road arrangement that looks like a
   four-leaf clover permits traffic to flow easily between
   two intersecting high-speed expressways.

10. The hippopotamus has a stout hairless body very short legs and a large head and muzzle.

11. Contrary to popular belief the tarantula a large hairy spider is not highly venomous.

12. Before a student can understand the principles of quantum physics he must master simple algebra.

13. While William Faulkner was writing his novel *As I Lay Dying* he worked in a Mississippi power plant.

14. Seeing a nightingale for the first time is disappointing; hearing one for the first time unforgettable.

15. History one would think ought to teach men not to make the same mistakes over again.

Exercise 6

Add necessary commas.

Ever since the earliest civilizations the seacoast has held great appeal to man and he has concentrated his habitations in that narrow belt which lies directly landward from the edge of the ocean. The coast has attracted man — ancient and modern — because it has provided a source of food and of that vital mineral salt. Climatically the coasts of the world are preferable to the interior because of the amelioration of the climate that comes from the much less variable ocean temperatures. The slow cooling of the ocean in winter keeps the coast warmer and the slow heating in summer keeps it cooler. Most coastal belts have a higher rainfall due to the nearby source of water and the onshore winds caused by heating of the land and the resulting convection currents.

Presumably early man was not particularly influenced by the esthetic beauty of the coasts; but going back as far as the time of the early Greeks man has given this factor great weight in choosing sites for his homes and temples. Finally with the development of the automobile there has been a tremendous growth of coastal highways. Because the public desires to look at beautiful scenery our own western seaboard has an almost continuous highway extending along the coast from Mexico to the Strait of Juan de Fuca which separates Washington and British Columbia. Coast routes along the East and Gulf Coasts are far less continuous partly because of the intricate indentations that push the roads inland and partly because of the low swampy lands and shifting belts of sand dunes.

ADAPTED FROM FRANCIS P. SHEPARD AND HAROLD R. WANLESS, *Our Changing Coastlines*

Exercise 7

Add necessary commas.

In my younger and more vulnerable years my father

gave me some advice that I've been turning over in my mind ever since.

"Whenever you feel like criticizing any one" he told me "just remember that all the people in this world haven't had the advantages that you've had."

He didn't say any more but we've always been unusually communicative in a reserved way and I understood that he meant a great deal more than that. In consequence I'm inclined to reserve all judgments a habit that has opened up many curious natures to me and also made me the victim of not a few veteran bores. The abnormal mind is quick to detect and attach itself to this quality when it appears in a normal person and so it came about that in college I was unjustly accused of being a politician because I was privy to the secret griefs of wild unknown men. Most of the confidences were unsought — frequently I have feigned sleep preoccupation or a hostile levity when I realized by some unmistakable sign that an intimate revelation was quivering on the horizon; for the intimate revelations of young men or at least the terms in which they express them are usually plagiaristic and marred by obvious suppressions. Reserving judgments is a matter of infinite hope. I am still a little afraid of missing something if I forget that as my father snobbishly suggested

and I snobbishly repeat a sense of the fundamental de-
cencies is parcelled out unequally at birth.

ADAPTED FROM F. SCOTT FITZGERALD, *The Great Gatsby*

Exercise 8

Add necessary commas.

The chief deity of the Aegeans was—like that of many
Asiatic cults—feminine. She was the *Great Goddess* the
Universal Mother in whom were united all the attributes
and functions of divinity. Above all she symbolised fertili-
ty and her influence extended over plants and animals as
well as humans. All the universe was her domain. As ce-
lestial goddess she regulated the course of the heavenly
bodies and controlled the alternating seasons. On earth
she caused the products of the soil to flourish gave men
riches protected them in battle and at sea guided them on
their adventurous voyages. She killed or tamed fierce
beasts; and finally she also reigned over the Underworld.

The Great Goddess is represented depending on the
epoch either crouching or standing. Sometimes she is
nude sometimes dressed like a Cretan woman. In the lat-
ter case she wears a flounced skirt and her bosom is either entirely bare or covered with a corsage which leaves
her breasts exposed. Her head-dress varies: the hair may

be free knotted with a simple fillet; it may be covered by a sort of turban decorated with flowers or aigrettes or by a conical tiara in the Oriental manner or again by a very tall tiara in the shape of a topless cone.

Although the type is always the same and only the attributes and details of dress vary it is questionable if a single divinity is concerned; on the contrary these various representations may well depict distinct goddesses each having her own character.

What was the name of the mother-goddess of the Aegeans? Here again in the absence of documentation we are left to conjecture. It seems that she was worshipped in Crete under the name *Rhea*. At least this was the name later associated with the ancient Cretan divinity in the cult of Zeus. Zeus was said to be her son—a tradition which Hesiod was to revive in his *Theogony*.

ADAPTED FROM FELIX GUIRANDS, *Greek Mythology*

21 Unnecessary Commas 𝓤𝓸 ,

Do not use excessive commas.

A comma at every possible pause within a sentence is not necessary. Generally it is better to use too little punctuation than too much.

21a Do not use a comma between subject and verb, between verb or verbal and complement, or between an adjective or adverb and the word it modifies.

NOT   The guard with the drooping mustache, snapped to attention.

The colonel said, that he had never seen such discipline.

Some students in the class, admitted, that they had not read, "Kubla Khan."

The stubborn, mischievous, child refused to respond.

BUT   The guard with the drooping mustache snapped to attention.

OR   The guard, the one with a drooping mustache, snapped to attention. (Two commas are correct with an intervening element.)

21b Do not use a comma between two compound elements, such as verbs, subjects, complements, or predicates except for contrast or emphasis.

UNNECESSARY   He *left* the scene of the accident, and *tried* to forget that it had happened.

See §20h for use of commas for contrast or emphasis.

21c Do not use a comma before a coordinating conjunction joining two dependent clauses except for contrast or emphasis.

UNNECESSARY   The contractor testified that the house was completed, and that the work had been done properly.

See §20a for the use of commas to separate independent clauses.

21d Do not use a comma before *than* in a comparison or between compound conjunctions like *as . . . as, so . . . as, so . . . that.*

AVOID John Holland was more delighted with life on the Continent, than he had thought he could be.

21e Do not use a comma after *like, such as*, and similar expressions.

A comma is used before *such as* only when the phrase is nonrestrictive.

comma here   *not* here
Some languages, such as Latin and Anglo-Saxon, are still studied but no longer spoken.

21f Do not use a comma with a period, a question mark, an exclamation point, or a dash. These marks stand by themselves.

AVOID "Did you get the job?", her roommate asked.

21g A comma may be used after a parenthesis, but not before.

no comma here
When he had finished reading *The Pilgrim's Progress* (the
comma here
most popular allegory in the language), he turned next to
The House of the Seven Gables.

21h A comma is not required after most short essential introductory adverbial modifiers or coordinating conjunctions.

NOT After he had slept, he felt more confident.

NOT Thus, he passed the examination.

NOT But, some people are excessively tolerant.

See §20d for the use of the comma after a long introductory clause or phrase.

21i Do not use commas to set off restrictive clauses, phrases, or appositives.

NOT People, who live in glass houses, should not throw stones.

See §20e.

21j Do not use a comma between adjectives which are not coordinate.

FAULTY The tired, old, work horse.

See §20c.

Exercise 9

Circle all unnecessary commas and be prepared to explain your decisions.

It is possible, to get an education at a university. It has been done; not often, but the fact that a proportion, however, small, of college students do get a start in interested, methodical study, proves my thesis, and the two, personal experiences I have to offer illustrate it, and show how to circumvent the faculty, the other students, and the whole, college system of mind-fixing. My method might lose a boy his degree, but a degree is not worth so much as the capacity, and the drive to learn, and the undergraduate desire, for an empty baccalaureate is one of the holds the educational system has, on students. Wise students some day will refuse to take degrees, as the best men (in England, for instance) give, but do not themselves accept, titles.

My method was hit on by accident, and some instinct. I specialized. With several courses prescribed, I concentrated on the one or two that interested me most, and letting the others go, I worked intensively, on my favorites. In my first two years, for example, I worked at English, and political economy, and read philosophy. At the beginning of my junior year, I had several cinches in history. Now, I liked history; I had neglected it, partly because I rebelled at the way it was taught, as positive knowledge unrelated to politics, art, life, or anything else. The professors gave us chapters out of a few books to read, con, and be quizzed on. Blessed as I was with a "bad memory," I could not commit to it anything, that I did not understand, and intellectually need. The bare record of the story of man, with names, dates, and irrelative events, bored me. But I had discovered in my readings of literature, philosophy, and political economy, that history had light to throw upon unhistorical questions. So, I proposed in my junior and senior years to specialize in history, taking all the courses required, and those also that I had flunked in. With this in mind I listened attentively to the first, introductory talk of Professor William Cary Jones on American, constitutional history. He was a dull lecturer, but I noticed that, after telling us what pages of what books we must be prepared in, he mumbled off some other references, "for those that may care to dig deeper."

ADAPTED FROM LINCOLN STEFFENS, Autobiography

22 The Semicolon ;

The semicolon (a stronger separator than the comma) is used between coordinate elements not otherwise connected.

It is mainly used between closely related independent clauses which balance or contrast with each other. Failure to use a semicolon may result in a comma splice or a fused sentence. See § 2.

22a Use a semicolon between two independent clauses not connected by a coordinating conjunction (*and, but, or, nor, for, so, yet*).

A semicolon is also used when the second independent clause is introduced by a conjunctive adverb (*however, therefore, moreover, then, consequently*) or by a sentence modifier (*in fact, in the first place, for example, on the other hand*).

WITH NO CONNECTIVE

For fifteen years the painting stood in the attic; even Mr. Kirk forgot it.

"It needed cleaning, and the frame was cracked," he explained later; "we just stored it away."

WITH A CONJUNCTIVE ADVERB

In 1970 a specialist from the museum arrived and asked to examine it; then all the family became excited.

WITH A SENTENCE MODIFIER

The painting was valuable; in fact, the museum offered five thousand dollars for it.

22b Use a semicolon between carefully balanced independent clauses for emphasis or contrast, even when they are connected by a coordinating conjunction.

Autocratic power springs from the will of the ruler; but democratic power rises from the will of the people.

22c Use a semicolon to separate independent clauses which are long and complex or which have internal punctuation.

In many compound sentences either a semicolon or a comma may be used.

COMMA OR   *Moby-Dick,* by Melville, is an adventure story, [*or;*]
SEMICOLON   and it is also one of the world's great philosophical novels.

SEMICOLON   Ishmael, the narrator, goes to sea, he says, "whenever
PREFERRED   it is a damp, drizzly November" in his soul; and Ahab, the captain of the ship, goes to sea because of his obsession to hunt and kill the great albino whale, Moby Dick.

22d Use semicolons in a series between items which have internal punctuation.

Gluttons like three times of day best: breakfast, when they can eat; lunch, when they can eat again; and dinner, when they can really eat.

22e Do not use a semicolon between elements which are not coordinate.

              dependent clause   *independent clause*
FAULTY   After he had signaled to his friend twice; he gave up and left the library.

Exercise 10

Circle unnecessary semicolons and commas and insert necessary ones. Write C to the left of sentences which are correct.

1. In Greek mythology Proteus was a sea god; one that could change his shape, whenever he wished.

2. The stipulations of the agreement were; that each company would keep its own name that profits would be evenly divided and that, no employee would lose his job; because of the merger.

3. From the thirty-third floor the people below; the automobiles; and the small buildings gave the effect of a world of toys and as the sun went down the lights below looked as if they were almost as far away as the stars.

4. An advanced civilization is guided by enlightened self-interest; however, it is also marked by unselfish good will.

5. Nothing is more annoying when one is trying to study than to have to listen to the noise of some unthinking idler; tapping his pencil on the table; humming under his breath; or talking and laughing with the girl sitting next to him.

6. The sound of the banjo drifted up from the floor below, it blended with the chatter of typewriters; and the droning of business conferences.

7. A child's first experience in the water is extremely important; if he enjoys this experience he may easily

learn to swim; and he will probably enjoy the water throughout his life.

8. No man likes to suffer; but through suffering man comes to understand more about life and death.

9. The Spanish Inquisition, which began as far back as the thirteenth century; kept better jails than the civil authorities, fed its prisoners more plentifully, and tortured its victims with far less severity than most people, those who have not studied the subject, believe.

10. Gambling creates in a person a deep sense of excitement even when he realizes that he cannot win; he will continue to gamble, driven by some profound impulse.

23 The Colon :

Use the colon as a formal and emphatic mark of introduction.

23a Use a colon before quotations, statements, and series which are introduced formally.

Sock and Buskin announces the opening of the following plays: *King Lear*, May 10; *The Circle*, June 14; and *Death of a Salesman*, July 19.

A quotation may be formally introduced without a verb of saying (*says, replies, remarks*).

The toastmaster made a brief talk: "Gentlemen, too many speeches are made in our world. Let's not have one tonight."

23b Use a colon between two independent clauses when the second explains or amplifies the first.

Music is more than something mechanical: it is an expression of deep feeling and ethical values.

23c Use a colon before formal appositives, including those introduced by such expressions as *namely* and *that is*.

There are three sources of belief: reason, custom, inspiration.
BLAISE PASCAL

One element is missing from some contemporary styles: good taste.

Note that the colon comes before *namely* and similar expressions, not after.

After a sleepless night the senator reached his decision: namely, that he would not seek re-election.

23d Use a colon between hours and minutes to indicate time, after the salutation of a formal letter, and between city and publisher in bibliographical entries.

12:15 P.M.
Dear Dr. Tyndale:
Boston: Houghton, 1929

23e Do not use a colon after a linking verb or a preposition.

FAULTY Some chief noise-makers are: automobiles, airplanes, and lawn mowers.

FAULTY His partner accused him of: talking too much during the game and not remembering what had been played.

24 The Dash /—

Use a dash to indicate interruptions, informal breaks in construction, parenthetical remarks, special emphasis, and to introduce summaries.

Distinguish carefully between the hyphen (-) and the dash (—). In longhand a dash should be about twice as long as a hyphen. In typescript a dash is made by two hyphens (--) with no space before or after.

FOR SUDDEN INTERRUPTIONS

He replied, "I will consider the— No, I won't either."

FOR SPECIAL EMPHASIS

Great authors quote one book more than any other— the Bible.

His suit— a psychedelic green— was the last thing I would have expected.

FOR SUMMARY

Attic fans, window fans, air conditioners— all were ineffective that summer.

25 Parentheses ( )

Use parentheses to enclose loosely related comment or explanation within a sentence and to enclose figures numbering items in a series.

The oil company refused to buy the land (1) because the owner had no clear title to the property and (2) because it was too far from the company's other wells.

The oil well (the company had drilled it only as an experiment) produced a thousand barrels a day.

Although the company had not expected a significant yield from the new well (they had drilled it only as an experiment), it produced a thousand barrels a day.

Mary McCauley (1754?–1832) was called Molly Pitcher because she used a pitcher to carry water to wounded soldiers.

A parenthetical sentence within another sentence does not end with a period. But when an entire free-standing sentence is enclosed in parentheses, the period comes *inside* the closing parenthesis.

Here are some useful RULES OF THUMB:

Use **parentheses** to enclose loosely connected parenthetical material.

Use **commas** to set off closely connected parenthetical material.

Use **dashes** to set off material to be dramatically emphasized.

Use **colons** to introduce a formal appositive, a list, or a quotation at the end of a sentence.

26 Square Brackets [ ]

Use square brackets to enclose interpolations in quotations.

In the opinion of Arthur Miller, "There is no more reason for falling down in a faint before his [Aristotle's] *Poetics* than before Euclid's geometry."

Sometimes a parenthesis within a parenthesis is enclosed in square brackets: ([ ]). Usually it is best to avoid a construction which calls for this punctuation.

27 Quotation Marks "/"

Use quotation marks to enclose the exact words of a speaker or writer and to set off some kinds of titles.

Most American writers and publishers use double quotation marks (". . .") except for internal quotations, which are set off by single quotation marks ('. . .'). See §27b.

27a Use quotation marks to enclose direct quotations and dialogue.

DIRECT QUOTATION At a high point in *King Lear*, the Duke of Gloucester says, "As flies to wanton boys, are we to the gods."

In dialogue a new paragraph marks each change of speaker.

DIALOGUE "What is fool's gold?" the explorer asked.
"Really," the geologist told him, "it's pyrites, which have the color of gold."

When a quotation of two or more paragraphs is not set

off in blocked style, quotation marks begin each paragraph but close only the last one.

In typescript, indent and single-space quotations other than dialogue which are more than about one hundred words long. Quotation marks are not used to enclose quotations blocked this way. (See p. 298.)

Poetry is single-spaced and centered between the left and right margins.

> If you would keep your soul
> From spotted sight or sound,
> Live like the velvet mole;
> Go burrow underground.

Short quotations of poetry may be run in with the text, not set off. They are then put in quotation marks, and a slash is used between lines.

Elinor Wylie satirically advises, "Live like the velvet mole;/Go burrow underground."

27b **Use single quotation marks to enclose a quotation within a quotation.**

The review explained: "Elinor Wylie is ironic when she advises, 'Live like the velvet mole.'"

27c **Use quotation marks to enclose the titles of essays, articles, short stories, short poems, chapters (and other subdivisions of books or periodicals), paintings, and short musical compositions.**

D. H. Lawrence's "The Rocking-Horse Winner" is a story about the need for love.

Chapter VII of *Walden* is entitled "The Beanfield." (For titles of books see §30a.)

A cheap reproduction of Van Gogh's "Sunflowers" hung on the wall above her desk.

NOTE: Do not use quotation marks around the title of your own theme in title position on your first page.

27d Do not use quotation marks to defend or emphasize slang, colloquialisms, or attempts at humor.

>   *avoid*
> The only way to treat a "weirdo" is to accept him.

27e Follow established conventions in placing other marks of punctuation with quotation marks.

Periods and **commas** are placed *inside* quotation marks in American usage.

All of the students had read "Lycidas."
"Amazing," the professor said.

Semicolons and **colons** are always placed *outside* closing quotation marks.

The customer wrote that he was "not yet ready to buy the first edition"; it was too expensive.

Thomas Wolfe referred to three geographical areas as "Dark Helen": the South, New England, and Germany.

A **question mark** or an **exclamation point** is placed *inside* quotation marks only when the quotation itself is a direct question or an exclamation. Otherwise, these marks are placed *outside*.

He asked, "Who is she?" (Only the quotation is a question.)

"Who is she?" he asked. (Only the quotation is a question.)

Did he ask, "Who is she?" (The quotation and the entire sentence are questions.)

Did he say, "I know her"? (The entire sentence asks a question; the quotation makes a statement.)

She screamed, "Run!" (Only the quotation is an exclamation.)

Curse the man who whispers, "No"! (The entire statement is an exclamation; the quotation is not.)

After quotations, never use a comma and an exclamation point or a question mark together.

NOT   "Help!," I cried.
NOT   "Help!", I cried.
BUT   "Help!" I cried.

28   End Punctuation   . / ? / !

End a declarative sentence with a period, an interrogative sentence with a question mark, and an exclamatory sentence with an exclamation point.

These marks of punctuation also have special uses within a sentence.

28a Use a period after a sentence which makes a statement or expresses a command.

Some modern women claim to be witches.

Water the flowers.

The gardener asked whether the plant should be taken indoors in winter. (This sentence is a statement even though it expresses an indirect question.)

28b Use periods after most abbreviations.

Periods follow such abbreviations as Mr., Dr., Pvt., Ave., B.C., A.M., Ph.D., e.g., ibid., and many others.

Abbreviations of governmental and international agencies often are written without periods: FCC, TVA, UNESCO, NATO, HEW, and so forth. Usage varies. When in doubt, consult your dictionary.

A comma or another mark of punctuation may follow the period after an abbreviation, but at the end of a sentence only one period is used.

After he earned his M.A., he began studying for his Ph.D.

But if the sentence is a question or an exclamation, the end punctuation mark follows the period after the abbreviation.

When does he expect to get his Ph.D.?

28c Use three spaced periods (ellipsis) to show omission in a quotation.

Notice how the source is shortened with ellipsis marks in the quotation that follows:

SOURCE
"He [the Indian] had no written record other than pictographs, and his conqueror was not usually interested, at the time, in writing down his thoughts and feelings for him. The stoic calm of his few reported speeches and poems gives only a hint of the rich culture that was so soon forgotten."

ROBERT E. SPILLER

QUOTATION WITH ELLIPSIS

Ellipsis not necessary at beginning of quotation.

The Indian "had no written record other than picto-

Three periods for ellipsis and one to end sentence.

graphs. . . . The stoic calm of his . . . speeches and poems gives

Three periods for ellipsis.

only a hint of the rich culture. . . ."

Four at end of sentence.

28d Do not put a period after the title of a theme, book, or periodical, but a question mark or an exclamation point may be part of a title.

> *The Sound and the Fury*   "What Are Years?"
> *Westward Ho!*   *Ah! Wilderness*

28e Use a question mark after a direct question.

Do teachers file attendance reports?

Teachers do file attendance reports? (A question in the form of a declarative sentence.)

Question marks may follow separate questions within a single interrogative sentence.

Do you recall the time of the accident? the license numbers of the cars involved? the names of the drivers? the names of the witnesses?

28f Use a question mark within parentheses to show that a date or a figure is doubtful.

Pythagoras, who died in 497 B.C. (?), was a mathematician.

Do not use a question mark or an exclamation point within a sentence to indicate humor or sarcasm. Be exact; rewrite the sentence.

NOT The comedy (?) was a miserable failure.

28g Use an exclamation point after a word, a phrase, or a sentence to signal strong exclamatory feeling.

Wait! I forgot my lunch!
Stop the bus!
What a ridiculous idea!

Use exclamation points sparingly. After mild exclamations use commas or periods.

NOT Well! I was discouraged!

BUT Well, I was discouraged.

Exercise 11

Supply quotation marks as needed in the following passage, and indicate new paragraphs where necessary by inserting the sign ¶.

Alex Tilman, young, vigorous, and alert, walked briskly beside the little stream. As he neared the pond, which the diligent beavers had made generations before, he thought of Thoreau's essay Walking and the sense of calm that pervaded nature. An old man was fishing with a pole on the bank of the pond. Knowing that fishermen dislike noise-makers, Alex strolled quietly up to the old man and said, How's your luck today? Oh, about like every other day, except a little worse, maybe. Do you mean you haven't caught anything? Well, I did catch a couple of bream. But they're small, you know. Before I left home my wife said to me, If you don't catch any sizable fish today, you might as well give it up. And I'm beginning to wonder if she hasn't got something there. Alex watched the water for a little while, now and then stealing a glance at the unshaved fisherman, who wore baggy breeches, a faded old flannel shirt, and a slouchy hat. Then he dreamily said, Well, I guess most people don't really fish just for the sake of catching something. The old gentleman looked up at him a little surprised. His eyes were much brighter and quicker than Alex had expected. That's right, he said, but, you know, that's not the kind of wisdom you hear these days from young folks. You new around here, son? Yes. My wife and I just bought the old Edgewright place. Oh. Well, maybe you can come fishing with me sometime. I'm usually around about this time during the day. Alex was not anxious to accept an invitation from a creature quite so shabby as this one, but he was moved by a sudden sympathy. Yes. Maybe. Say, if you need any work, I might be able to find something for you to do around our place. My wife and I are trying to get things cleaned up. A slight smile came over the old fellow's face, and he said warmly, Much obliged, but I've got more work now than I know what to do with. So I come out here and hum Lazy Bones and fish. On the way back to his house, Alex asked a neighbor who that old tramp was fishing down by the pond. Tramp! his friend repeated. Good heavens, man, that was no tramp. That was Angus Morgan, one of the wealthiest men in the county.

Exercise 12

Add quotation marks where needed; circle unnecessary ones. Also make all necessary changes in punctuation. Where new paragraphs are needed insert the sign ¶.

1. "Failure is often necessary for humanity", Professor Xavier said. Without failure, he continued, how can we retain our humility and know the full sweetness of success? For, as Emily Dickinson said: Success is counted sweetest/ By those who ne'er succeed.

2. Madam, said the talent scout, I know that you think your daughter can sing, but, believe me, her voice makes the strangest sounds I have ever heard. Mrs. Audubon took her daughter "Birdie" by the hand and haughtily left the room wondering "how she could ever have been so stupid as to expose her daughter to such a 'common' person."

3. Your assignment for tomorrow, said Mrs. Osborn, is to read the following (to use Poe's own term) tales of ratiocination: The Purloined Letter, The Murders in the Rue Morgue, and The Mystery of Marie Roget; when you have finished these stories you might read ahead into the next assignment.

4. The boy and his great-uncle were "real" friends, and the youngster listened intently when the old man spoke. Son, he would say, I remember my father's words: You can't do better than to follow the advice of Ben Franklin, who said, One To-day is worth two To-morrows.

5. The expression population explosion suggests the extreme rapidity with which the world's "population" is increasing.

6. A recent report states the following: The marked increase in common stocks indicated a new sense of national security; however, the report seems to imply "that this is only one of many gauges of the country's economic situation."

7. Chapter IV, The National Mind, is one of the most optimistic views of the country's future to be found in "modern" studies of economics.

8. One of Mark Twain's most famous letters, addressed to "Andrew Carnegie," reads as follows:

    "You seem to be in prosperity. Could you lend an admirer $1.50 to buy a hymn-book with? God will bless you. I feel it; I know it. So will I."

    "N.B.—If there should be other applications, this one not to count".

9. In a "postscript," Mark Twain added, Don't send the hymn-book; send the money; I want to make the selection myself. He signed the letter simply Mark.

10. The conversation between Aunt Hattie and the door-to-door salesman went something like this. Madam, you have been very highly recommended to us. As an

advertising venture, will you allow us to put a set of these books in your home? No. But I don't think you understand. No. What I mean is, there is no charge at all for— No. For the books themselves. No! Good-day, young man. Slam!

Mechanics

Make your papers neat and inviting to read. Misspellings and wrong capitalization and other errors in mechanics may detract from even excellent thought.

29 Manuscript and Letter Form *ms*

Follow correct manuscript form in your papers and business letters.

Themes For themes and other course papers use white paper 8½ by 11 inches for typescript, ruled paper for longhand. Do not use onionskin. Use blue or black ink. When typing, double-space. In longhand it is neater to skip every other line. Write or type on one side of the paper only. Center the title and leave extra space between title and text.

Leave ample and regular margins at the top and bottom of the page, and leave at least an inch on each side.

Indent the first line of each paragraph uniformly—about one inch in longhand and five spaces in typescript.

Example of Correct Manuscript Form

THE BLUFFTON HOUSE ◄——— Center

◄—— Triple space

┌— Indent 5 spaces

Double-space

2 spaces after periods

To me, Bluffton Farm is synonymous with vacation time, and its outstanding feature is the forty-year-old house. It sits back in a grove of pines and palmettos, looking like an ugly duckling between the modern, two-story brick houses of my aunt and uncle. It is built of heart-of-pine lumber, which has no paint--and never has had. A once-red roof covers the long structure. └—— 2 hyphens and no spaces for a dash

A rusted screen porch, which runs the full length of the house, is notable by itself. It is furnished with Army surplus cots covered with khaki cloth, and it has eight bright green rocking chairs with deerskin bottoms. The cots are lined up like prone bodies under the windows of the bedrooms, and the rocking chairs seem to keep watch over the river in front of the house. The porch is a marvelous place for wet swimmers to lounge, and the dirt which clings to bathing suits cannot hurt the furniture. In the middle of the porch floor is a crack about two inches wide. Dirt and sand are swept into this crack, and a pile of dirt under the house is evidence of many years of living and sweeping.

Behind the porch is the dining room, a very utilitarian place about thirty feet long with a homemade table about twenty feet long. Layers and layers of oilcloth cover the table, and during family reunions I have seen twenty people sit down there

1 ◄——— Page number for first page on bottom line

Number all pages except the first with an Arabic numeral in the upper right corner: 2, *not* II. On the first page the number should be omitted or centered at the bottom of the page.

Before submitting any paper, read over the final draft two or three times, at least once aloud for sound. (For method of revising, see pp. xviiff.) If possible, allow a period of time between readings. Watch especially for misspellings, typographical errors, punctuation, and omissions made in revising or copying.

Revising and correcting papers after they have been read and marked by your instructor is often required and always helpful.

Business Letters   In writing a business letter follow the conventional form. All essential parts are included in the example on p. 128. The letter should be typewritten if possible, single-spaced, with double-spacing (i.e., one blank line) between paragraphs. Paragraphs may be indented or may begin at the left margin without indentation.

Business letters are usually written on stationery 8½ by 11 inches. Fold horizontally into thirds to fit a standard-sized business envelope. For smaller envelopes fold once horizontally and twice the other way.

30 Underlining and Italic Type   *ital*

Underline to represent italics in titles of independent publications (books, magazines, newspapers) and occasionally for emphasis.

Italic type slants (*like this*).
Underline words individually (<u>like</u> <u>this</u>).

A Business Letter and Envelope

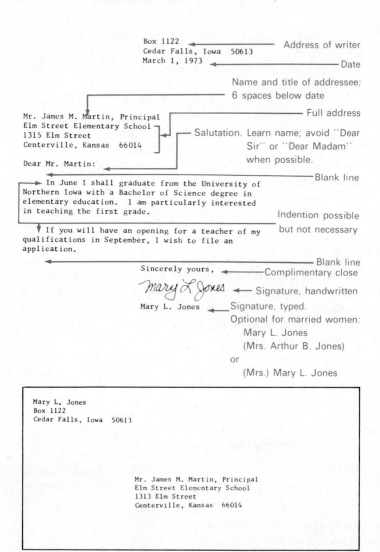

Box 1122
Cedar Falls, Iowa 50613 ← Address of writer
March 1, 1973 ← Date

Name and title of addressee;
6 spaces below date

Mr. James M. Martin, Principal ← Full address
Elm Street Elementary School
1315 Elm Street
Centerville, Kansas 66014

— Salutation. Learn name; avoid "Dear
Sir" or "Dear Madam"
when possible.

Dear Mr. Martin:

— Blank line

In June I shall graduate from the University of
Northern Iowa with a Bachelor of Science degree in
elementary education. I am particularly interested
in teaching the first grade.

Indention possible
but not necessary

If you will have an opening for a teacher of my
qualifications in September, I wish to file an
application.

— Blank line

Sincerely yours, ←— Complimentary close

Mary L Jones ← Signature, handwritten

Mary L. Jones ← Signature, typed.
Optional for married women:
Mary L. Jones
(Mrs. Arthur B. Jones)
or
(Mrs.) Mary L. Jones

Mary L. Jones
Box 1122
Cedar Falls, Iowa 50613

Mr. James M. Martin, Principal
Elm Street Elementary School
1313 Elm Street
Centerville, Kansas 66014

30a Underline titles of books (except the Bible and its divisions), periodicals, newspapers, motion pictures, television programs, musical compositions, plays, and other works published separately.

Be precise: watch initial articles (*A*, *An*, *The*) and any punctuation.

BOOKS   Adventures of Huckleberry Finn [not The Adventures . . .]
An American Tragedy [not The American Tragedy]

PERIODICALS   The Atlantic Monthly and the American Quarterly

NEWSPAPERS   New York Times

MOTION PICTURES   Citizen Kane

TELEVISION PROGRAMS   Sesame Street

MUSICAL COMPOSITIONS   Bizet's Carmen
Beethoven's Mount of Olives

PLAYS   The Cherry Orchard

NOTE: Do not underline the title of your own theme.

30b Underline names of ships and trains.

the Queen Elizabeth II   the U.S.S. Hornet   the Zephyr

30c Underline foreign words used in an English context, except words which have become part of our language.

Consult a dictionary to determine whether a word is still considered foreign or has become Anglicized.

> Fried grasshoppers were the <u>pièce de résistance</u> of the meal.

BUT

> 1899   1902   1902   1697   1880
>
> The chauffeur garaged the limousine with verve and élan. (The dates show when these words [all from French] came into English, according to the *Oxford English Dictionary*. Long accepted, they are not italicized or underlined.)

30d Underline words, letters, and figures referred to as such.

> The word *puppy* usually has delightful connotations.
> Don't forget to dot your *i*'s.

30e Avoid excessive underlining for emphasis.

Weak writing is seldom improved by mechanical tricks. Do not sprinkle a page with underlinings, dashes, or exclamation points.

31 Spelling *sp*

Spell correctly; use a dictionary to look up words you are unsure of.

Spelling is troublesome in English because many words are not spelled as they sound (*laughter*, *slaughter*); because some distinct pairs and triplets sound the same (*capital, capitol; there, their; to, too, two*); and because many words are pronounced with the vowel sound "uh," which gives no clue to spelling (sens*i*ble, cap*a*ble, def*i*ant).

Many misspellings are due to the omission of syllables in habitual pronunciations (*accident-ly* for *acciden-tal-ly*); the addition of syllables (*disas-ter-ous* for *disas-trous*); or the changing of syllables (p*r*espiration for p*e*rspiration).

There are no infallible guides to spelling in English, but the following are helpful.

i-e or e-i?

> Use *i* before *e*
> Except after *c*
> Or when sounded as *a*
> As in *neighbor* and *weigh*.

i-e

believe, chief, field, grief, piece

e-i

After *c*
    receive, receipt, ceiling, deceit, conceive

When sounded as *a*
    freight, vein, reign

EXCEPTIONS TO MEMORIZE:
    either, neither, leisure, seize, weird, height

Drop final silent e?

DROP

*When suffix begins with
a vowel*

curse	cursing
come	coming
pursue	pursuing
arrange	arranging
dine	dining

COMMON TYPICAL EXCEPTIONS
couraGEous
notiCEable
dyEing (compare *dying*)
singEing (compare *singing*)

KEEP

*When suffix begins with
a consonant*

live	lively
nine	ninety
hope	hopeful
love	loveless
arrange	arrangement

COMMON TYPICAL EXCEPTIONS
awful
ninth
truly
argument

Change y to i?

CHANGE

When y *is preceded by
a consonant*

gully	gullies
try	tried
fly	flies
apply	appliance, applied
party	parties

DO NOT CHANGE

When y *is preceded by
a vowel*

valley	valleys
attorney	attorneys
convey	conveyed
pay	pays
deploy	deploying

When adding -ing

try	trying
fly	flying
apply	applying

Double final consonant?

If the suffix begins with a consonant, do not double the final consonant of the base word: *man, manly.*

If the suffix begins with a vowel—

DOUBLE	DO NOT DOUBLE
When final consonant is preceded by single vowel	*When final consonant is preceded by two vowels*

	Monosyllables		
	pen	penned	despair	despairing
	blot	blotted	leer	leering

| despair | despairing |
| leer | leering |

Words ending with two or more consonants preceded by single vowel

| jump | jumping |
| work | working |

pen	penned
blot	blotted
hop	hopper
sit	sitting

Polysyllables accented on last syllable

defér	deferring
begín	beginning
omít	omitting
occúr	occurring

Polysyllables not accented on last syllable after addition of suffix

defér	déference
prefér	préference
devélop	devéloping
lábor	lábored

Add s or es?

ADD S	ADD ES
For plurals of most nouns	*When the plural has an extra syllable*

girl	girls	church	churches
book	books	fox	foxes

For nouns ending in o *preceded by a vowel*	*Usually for nouns ending in* o *preceded by a consonant (consult your dictionary when in doubt)*	
radio	radios	
cameo	cameos	potatoes
		Negroes

BUT flamingos or flamingoes
Filipinos

NOTE: The plurals of proper names are generally formed by adding *s* or *es*: *Darby*, the *Darbys*; *Delano*, the *Delanos*; *Jones*, the *Joneses*.

Words Frequently Misspelled

absence	analysis	ascend
accidentally	analyze	athletic
accommodate	annual	attendance
accumulate	apartment	balance
acquaintance	apparatus	battalion
acquitted	apparent	beginning
advice	appearance	believe
advise	arctic	benefited
amateur	argument	boundaries
among	arithmetic	Britain

business
calendar
candidate
category
cemetery
changeable
changing
choose
chose
commission
committee
comparative
coming
compelled
conceivable
conferred
conscience
conscientious
control
criticize
deferred
definite
description
desperate
dictionary
dining
disappearance
disappoint
disastrous
discipline
dissatisfied
dormitory
eighth
eligible
eliminate

embarrass
eminent
encouraging
environment
equipped
especially
exaggerate
excellence
exhilarate
existence
experience
explanation
familiar
fascinate
February
fiery
foreign
formerly
forty
fourth
frantically
generally
government
grammar
grandeur
grievous
height
heroes
hindrance
hoping
humorous
hypocrite
hypocrisy
immediately
incidentally

incredible
independence
inevitable
intellectual
intelligence
interesting
irresistible
knowledge
laboratory
laid
led
lightning
loneliness
maintenance
maneuver
manufacture
mathematics
may
maybe
miniature
mischievous
mysterious
necessary
Negroes
ninety
noticeable
occasionally
occurred
omitted
opportunity
optimistic
parallel
paralyze
pastime
performance

permissible	receive	statue
perseverance	recognize	truly
personnel	recommend	their
perspiration	reference	to
physical	referred	too
picnicking	repetition	succeed
possibility	restaurant	successful
practically	rhythm	supersede
precede	ridiculous	surprise
precedence	sacrifice	studying
preference	sacrilegious	temperamental
preferred	salary	tendency
prejudice	schedule	thorough
preparation	secretary	tragedy
prevalent	seize	tries
privilege	separate	tyranny
professor	sergeant	unanimous
pronunciation	severely	undoubtedly
prophecy	shining	until
prophesy	siege	usually
probably	similar	village
quantity	sophomore	villain
quiet	specifically	weather
quite	specimen	weird
quizzes	stationary	whether
recede	stationery	writing

32 The Hyphen and Syllabication /–

Use a hyphen in certain compound words and in words divided at the end of a line.

32a Consult a dictionary to determine whether a compound is hyphenated or written as one word or as two.

HYPHENATED	ONE WORD	TWO WORDS
one-way	droplight	drop leaf (noun)
white-hot	whitewash	white heat
water-cooled	watermelon	water system

32b Hyphenate a compound of two or more words used as a single modifier before a noun.

HYPHEN	NO HYPHEN AFTER NOUN
He is a *well-known* executive	The executive is *well known.*

A hyphen is not used when the first word of such a group is an adverb ending in *-ly.*

HYPHEN	NO HYPHEN
a *half-finished* task	a *partly finished* task

32c Hyphenate spelled-out compound numbers from *twenty-one* through *ninety-nine.*

32d Follow accepted syllabication in hyphenating a word at the end of a line.

When in doubt, consult a dictionary. Hyphenate only between syllables, and place the hyphen only at the end of the first line, not at the beginning of the next.

Do not divide monosyllables even if they are long (*thought, laugh, cheese*), and do not set off a single letter (*a-bout, might-y*). Prefixes and suffixes may be set off, though it is preferable not to carry over a two-letter suffix (*straight-ened,* not *straighten-ed*). Compounds normally written with a hyphen (*self-satisfied*) should not be divided elsewhere at the end of a line (not *self-satis-fied*).

33 The Apostrophe /'

Use the apostrophe to form the possessive case in many nouns, to form some plurals, and to show omission or contraction.

1. Use 's to form the possessive of nouns not ending in *s*.

SINGULAR   child's, man's, deer's, lady's, mother-in-law's
PLURAL   children's, men's

2. Use 's or apostrophe only for the possessive of singular nouns ending in *s*.

   Charles's, Watts's, Dickens's, waitress's, actress's

   NOTE: When 's added to a singular noun ending in *s* causes a difficulty in pronunciation, add only the apostrophe.

   the actress' success, Dickens' stories

3. Use ' without *s* to form the possessive of plural nouns ending in *s*.

   the Joneses' car, the Dickenses' home, waitresses' tips

4. Use 's to form the possessive of indefinite pronouns.

   anybody's, everyone's, somebody else's, neither's

   NOTE: Use no apostrophe with personal pronouns: *his, theirs, ours, its* (meaning *of it*). *It's* means *it is*.

5. Use 's with only the last noun to show joint possession in a pair or a series.

   Marge and Jack's bicycle (The two jointly own one bicycle.)
   Marge's and Jack's bicycles (Each owns his own bicycle.)

6. Use ' to mark omissions or contractions.

the roaring '20's, o'clock, jack-o'-lantern, we'll, don't, can't, it's (it is)

7. Use 's to form the plural of numerals, letters, and words referred to as words.

three 7's (but three sevens), four *a*'s, six *the*'s

34 Capital Letters *cap*

Use a capital letter to begin a sentence and to mark a proper noun — the name of a particular person, place, or thing.

Capitalize:

The first word of a sentence.

The pronoun *I*.

The interjection *O*.

How, O ye gods, can I bear this misfortune?

First, last, and important words in titles, even the second part of hyphenated words.

Across the River and into the Trees
"The Man Against the Sky"
"After Apple-Picking"

NOTE: Articles (*a, an, the*) and short prepositions and conjunctions are not capitalized unless they begin a title.

The first word of a direct quotation and words capitalized by the author.

Carlyle said, "Meanwhile, we will hate Anarchy as Death, which it is. . . . "

Titles preceding a name.

> President Truman

Titles of high rank.

> The President is not expected to veto the measure.

Titles used specifically as substitutes for particular names.

> Lieutenant Yo pleaded not guilty; the Lieutenant was found innocent.

> NOTE: A title not followed by a name is usually not capitalized.

> The stockholders sat down, and the president called for order.

Titles which are common nouns naming an office are not capitalized.

> A college president has more duties than privileges.
> A lieutenant deserves a good living allowance.

Degrees and titles after a name.

> Jeffrey E. Tyndale, Sr., Ph.D., J.D.
> Abraham Lincoln, Attorney at Law

> NOTE: Do not capitalize names of occupations used as appositives or as descriptions.

> Abraham Lincoln, a young lawyer from Springfield, took the case.

Words of family relationship used as names.

> After Father died, Mother carried on the business.

BUT   After my father died, my mother carried on the business.

Proper nouns and their derivatives.

	BUT
Plato, Platonic, Platonism	pasteurize
Venice, Venetian blind	a set of china
the West, a Westerner	west of the river
the Republican Party	a republican government
the Senior Class of Ivy College	a member of the senior class
Clifton Street	my street
the Mississippi River	the Mississippi and Ohio rivers

Months, days of the week, holidays.

> April, Friday, the Fourth of July, Labor Day

NOTE: Do not capitalize seasons and numbered days of the month unless they name holidays.

> spring, the third of July

Movements, periods, events in history.

> the Romantic Movement
> the Civil War

NOTE: Do not capitalize the name of a century as such.

> the twentieth century

B.C., A.D., words designating the Deity, religious denomi-nations, sacred books.

> in 273 B.C.
> the Messiah, our Maker, the Trinity, Allah, Buddha, Jesus, He
> "Praise God from Whom all blessings flow. Praise Him. . . . "
> Catholic, Protestant, Presbyterian
> the Bible, the Koran
> the Old Testament

NOTE: Pronouns referring to the Deity may or may not be capitalized.

> "Praise God from whom all blessings flow."

Names of specific courses.

> I registered for Sociology 101 and Chemistry 445.

NOTE: Do not capitalize studies (other than languages) which do not name specific courses.

> I am taking English, sociology, and chemistry.

35 Abbreviations *ab*

Use only acceptable abbreviations.

Abbreviations are short cuts. Some are accepted in all kinds of writing; others are not.

The following abbreviations are acceptable in all con-texts.

BEFORE A NAME	Mr., Mrs., Ms., Messrs., Mmes., Dr., St. or Ste. (for *Saint* not *Street*), Mt., Rev. (but only with a first name: "the Rev. Ernest Jones," not "Rev. Jones")

NOTE: In British usage, periods are often omitted after titles (*Mr*). This is not the practice in the United States.

AFTER A NAME	M.D. (and other degrees), Jr., Sr., Esq., D.C. (Washington, D.C.; but except in addresses spell out names of states and other geographical areas):
	I live in Massachusetts.
NOT	I live in Mass.
OTHERS	B.C. and A.D. (with dates expressed in numerals, as 500 B.C.)
	A.M. and P.M. (with hours expressed in numerals, as 4:00 A.M.)
FOOTNOTES AND BIBLI- OGRAPHIES	cf., pp., and others
UNITS OF MEASURE	cc., c., gr., and others

NOTE: In scientific and technical writing the metric abbreviations are commonly written without periods.

36 Numbers 𝓃𝓊𝓂

Spell out round numbers that can be written in one or two words.

twenty-three
one thousand
one thousand dollars

Use figures for other numbers.

123
$1^{13}/_{16}$
$1,001.00

EXCEPTIONS: Never use figures at the beginning of a sentence. Spell out the number or recast the sentence.

Use numerals for figures in a series and for tabulations and statistics:

> One polar bear weighed 200 pounds; another, 526; the third, 534.
>
> One coat sold for $200, one for $275, and one for $325.

Use figures for dates, street numbers, page references, percentages, and hours of the day used with A.M. or P.M.

USE FIGURES	SPELL OUT
July 3, 1776 [not 3d]	the third of July
3 July 1970	
1010 State Street	Fifth Avenue
See page 50.	The book has fifty pages.
He paid 8 per cent interest.	
The concert begins at 6 P.M. (or 6:00 P.M.)	The concert begins at six o'clock.

Diction and Style

Diction is choice of words. Style is manner of writing, the way a writer expresses his thoughts in language. Effective writing always involves the choice of words and expressions, the arrangement of words in sentences, and variety in the patterns of sentences. Sentences which express similar ideas may have vastly different effects, and much of the difference is a matter of style. The following examples are related in content but very dissimilar in detail and stylistic effect:

Time flies.

Time is infinite movement without one moment of rest.

TOLSTOY, *War and Peace*

How soon hath Time, the subtle thief of youth,
Stol'n on his wing my three and twentieth year.

JOHN MILTON

Dost thou love Life? Then do not squander time, for that is the stuff life is made of.

Poor Richard's Almanac

> It continues ever true . . . that Saturn, or Chronos, or what
> we call Time, devours all his Children: only by incessant
> Running, by incessant Working, may you (for some three-
> score-and-ten years) escape him; and you too he devours at
> last.
>
> THOMAS CARLYLE, *Sartor Resartus*

Writing may be whimsical, poetic, terse, flippant, imaginative, literal, and so on. Develop the habit of noticing
the style and tone of what you read and what you write.
Your own style should be appropriate to your subject and
to your own personality. Style is not simple adornment.
Although the quotations above denote attitudes toward
the passing of time, their connotations and the details of
their content differ widely. Style reflects thought, shapes
meaning, and expresses individuality. The kinds of writing
above vary from the terse to the longer, from the simple
to the complex, from the plain to the ornate and the figurative.

37 Standard English   *d*

**Use Standard English except on special occasions, and con-
sult your dictionary on questions of usage.**

The language in generally accepted use in the English-
speaking countries is known as **Standard English.** It may be
characterized as the language of educated persons.
Though it varies in some details from one country to another, as is indicated by such labels as *U.S.* or *Brit.* in dictionaries, it is the common language of the great majority
of those who communicate in English, and that is why it
is taught in schools and colleges. **Nonstandard,** corre-
spondingly, refers to usages, spellings, or pronunciations

not usually found in the speech or writing of educated persons.

Consult your dictionary for definitions of the status or usage labels it employs (e.g., *Slang, Dialect, Colloquial, Informal, Obsolete,* etc.). The best sources of information are dictionaries which record usage both current and past. The question is "What is appropriate?" rather than "What is correct?" A dictionary is not prescriptive; it does not tell you what is "right." Rather, it describes usage; it tells who uses what and lets you make your own choices. In minor matters dictionaries do not always agree. In current dictionaries, for example, you will find the forms *cooperate, co-operate,* and *coöperate.*

Particularly useful at the college level are the following desk dictionaries:

The American Heritage Dictionary of the English Language. New York: American Heritage Publishing Company, and Boston: Houghton Mifflin Company.

The Random House Dictionary of the English Language, College Edition. New York: Random House.

Standard College Dictionary. New York: Funk & Wagnalls Company. Text Edition. New York: Harcourt Brace Jovanovich.

Webster's New World Dictionary of the American Language. Cleveland: The World Publishing Company.

Webster's Seventh New Collegiate Dictionary. Springfield, Mass.: G. & C. Merriam Company.

37a Use slang only when nothing else will serve as well.

Slang, a colorful nonstandard language usually invented by special groups, has a vocabulary which changes constantly. The poet Carl Sandburg described it as "language that takes off its coat, spits on its hands, and gets to work." Nevertheless, it has real weaknesses. Its effectiveness depends on freshness and novelty; slang words soon wear out from overuse and become flabby and dated. But the main reason why college instructors object to the use of slang in student papers is that it is too often an easy, popular rubber stamp which only approximates exact thought, a lazy way of avoiding the effort to find an exact and really vivid word or phrase. A person who said "He's a jerk" would not communicate much. What precisely does this mean except that he is in some vague and unspecified way unattractive?

Another objection to slang in student papers is that it may turn out to be funny at the writer's expense. Slang expressions are particularly vulnerable when dropped innocently into a moderately formal context:

> The violin virtuoso's performance on the cello was a *real bomb*.

> When Macbeth recoiled at the thought of murder, Lady Macbeth urged him not to *chicken out*.

Yet slang which is vivid and useful often becomes Standard. "Skyscraper," "bus," and "mob" were once slang, and there simply is no other word that conveys quite the same meanings as "date."

37b Do not use dialect except to give the flavor of local speech. Avoid illiteracies.

Words and usages peculiar to one section of the country are **dialect**. In various regions, for example, a dragonfly is called a darning needle, a snake feeder, a snake doctor, and a mosquito hawk. In the same way, the speech and linguistic patterns of a particular social group, especially an ethnic minority, are often termed dialect.

There is no reason to erase all dialectal characteristics from language. They are a cultural heritage and a continuing source of richness, flavor, and variety. But in general communication it is wise to avoid expressions which are not widely understood or which reflect ignorance of standard usage.

For the same reason, **illiteracies**, which are found in the language of people who are unable to read and write, should be avoided in speech and writing.

NOT   She ain't ready yet. Would you care to set awhile?

37c Avoid archaic words.

Archaisms, out-of-date words, are often encountered in dialect and in literature. *Oft, yon*, and *holp* (past tense of *help*) are examples. They are seldom appropriate in modern speech or writing.

37d Avoid improprieties. Use words in their correct functions and meanings.

A **functional impropriety** is the use of a word in the wrong part of speech. Many nouns, for example, do not also serve as adjectives or verbs. Thus it is not Standard English to write *orchestra selection* for *selection by the orchestra* or *orchestral selection*. *Cliché* is a noun; *clichéd* would be an impropriety.

The wrong meaning for a word can also be an impropriety. See §37h.

The following list contains examples of the most common kinds of improprieties.

IMPROPRIETIES	PROPER FORMS
occupation hazards (noun for adjective)	*occupational* hazards
psychology approach (noun for adjective)	*psychological* approach
a *fantasy* play (noun for adjective)	a *fantasy*
suspicioned (noun made into verb)	*suspected*
satired the committee (noun made into verb)	*satirized* the committee
an *invite* (verb for noun)	an *invitation*
good *eats* (verb for noun)	good *eating* (or good *food*)
stagnate waters (verb for adjective)	*stagnant* waters
surprising great number (adjective for adverb)	*surprisingly* great number

37e Use correct idioms.

An idiom is a group of words combined into a fixed unit of language with an arbitrary meaning. Idioms seldom mean what they literally say. Such expressions as *how do you do, a man in his shirt sleeves, with the naked eye, step into a job, run for office, back down, back out, down and out,* and *every other day* cannot be translated or interpreted literally. Many English idioms are verb phrases, e.g., *put out, put out about* (or *by*), *put up, put in, put down. Differ from* means to be unlike; *differ with* means to disagree with. Many common errors in English idiom occur in the use of prepositions after verbs. A good dictionary lists idiomatic uses of all kinds.

Study the following list of common idioms.

UNIDIOMATIC	IDIOMATIC
angry at (a person)	angry with (a person)
cannot help but	cannot help
comply to	comply with
conform in	conform to (*or* with)
different than	different from
doubt if	doubt that, whether
ever now and then	every now and then
identical to	identical with
in accordance to	in accordance with
incapable to do	incapable of doing
in search for	in search of
intend on doing	intend to do
in the year of 1970	in the year 1970
off of	off
on a whole	on the whole
plan on	plan to
similar with	similar to
superior than	superior to
try and see	try to see
type of a	type of

37f **Avoid specialized vocabulary in writing for the general reader.**

For most purposes it is best to keep your language clear and plain. Every specialist from cook to engineer to philosopher has his own vocabulary. Some specialized words find their way into general use; most do not. We know the plastic *lucite*, but not its chemical name, the acrylic resin *polymethyl methacrylate.*

Trouble comes when the specialist either cannot or does not see the need to express his ideas in language for the general reader. The following passage, for instance, is addressed to a limited group, for it can be understood only by the person who knows the technical terms used:

> Whenever an effector activity (R) is closely associated with a stimulus afferent impulse or trace (s) and the conjunction is closely associated with the rapid diminution in the motivational stimulus (S_D or S_G), there will result an increment ($\triangle$) to a tendency for that stimulus to evoke that response.
> CLARK L. HULL, *A Behavior System*

Contrast the foregoing passage with the following, in which technical terms are held to a minimum and the needs of the general reader are kept in mind:

> Investigators began to look more than 50 years ago for the dreaded invader of the central nervous system now identified as the polio virus. Once they had isolated the virus and learned to work with it in the laboratory, they made an unexpected discovery. The virus turns up much more often in the intestinal tract than it does in the spinal cord and brain. In human beings the infection usually goes unnoticed, causing no harm and conferring a lasting immunity; only occasionally does it involve the nervous system and bring on serious illness. The tracing of the polio virus to its habitat in the gut has led more recently to the discovery that it is a member of a large family of viruses. They all produce the same sort of benign infection in the alimentary tract, and exhibit the same tendency to invade other tissues, especially the nervous system, with more serious consequences. The so-called enteroviruses now number more than 50. Some have proved to be agents of hitherto mysterious diseases. Although other members of the family have not yet been incriminated, they re-

main under close surveillance, for there are a number of diseases that have no known cause, and the enteroviruses have not been eliminated as suspects.

JOSEPH L. MELNICK, "Enteroviruses"

Except for the terms *polio* and *virus*, generally well known, the only technical term in the passage is *enteroviruses* (intestinal viruses), whose meaning can in part be deduced from the context. Special vocabularies may obscure meaning. Moreover, they tempt the writer into the use of inflated and vague words instead of plain ones—a style sometimes known as *gobbledygook* or *governmentese* because it flourishes in bureaucratic writing. Thus A. P. Herbert has suggested that Lord Nelson's famous Trafalgar message ("England expects every man to do his duty") would be written in modern gobbledygook as follows: "England anticipates that as regards the current emergency personnel will face up to the issues and exercise appropriately the functions allocated to the respective occupation groups."

Exercise 1

Many of the following expressions can be used at more than one level of style or usage, depending on context. Select ten; identify each with an appropriate label— Standard, Nonstandard, Formal, Informal, Colloquial, Slang, *etc. (Note: There is no universal system of usage labels. Read the preliminary pages in your dictionary and be sure you understand its particular system. Combine the use of your dictionary with your own judgment.)*

angry

beak (nose)

blockhead

bunk (to occupy a bed)

bunk (nonsense)
clove (past tense)
drag race
edifice
enthuse
Erin
erstwhile (formerly)
exam
fardel
faux pas
feist
flu
freak (an enthusiast)
fresh (presumptuous)
the glim
gobbledygook
goofy
greenhorn
hen (a woman)
high-hat

hussy
idiomatic
in-depth
kine (cows)
loco (insane)
loser (a failure)
mad (angry)
octane
off the beam
pep
pinkie
rattle (to confuse)
shades (sunglasses)
shipshape
sidle
steed
sunglasses
traumatic
turn turtle
y-clept

37g Avoid triteness. Strive for fresh and original expressions.

Cliches are stock phrases and figures of speech once striking but used so often that they have lost their suggestive value. _A bull in a china shop_ was once vivid and funny, but it has been used so many times that we no longer visualize the careening animal and the flying porcelain. Examples of triteness are innumerable: _it is interesting to note, flat as a flounder, pandemonium reigned, true blue,_

*apple of his eye, tired but happy, quick as lightning, quick
as a flash, an ax to grind,* and so forth.

37h Be exact. Use words in their precise meanings.

Knowledge of idiom, use of a dictionary, and awareness of
the ways words are used—all of these are necessary for
precision in writing. The misuse of a word like *preserva-
tion* for the more exact *conservation* results in vagueness
and confusion. Correct use of words derives from good
habits with language rather than from rules. The misused words in the following sentences express wrong
meanings.

> She was *overtaken* by the heat.
> (*Overcome* was intended.)

> And *foremost*, both librarians lost their patience.
> (Was *immediately* intended? Or *first?*)

> She *parallels* the love she feels with the permanence of the tree.
> (*Compares* would be better.)

Misuse of one word for another that is somewhat like it
can make a sentence ridiculous.

> A few *extractions* from the book will prove the point.
> (The word is *extracts*.)

> Hamlet wished to get *avenge* for the murder of his father.
> (*Revenge*.)

> As the sun beams down upon the swamp, no different varieties
> of color are reflected, only the unreal grayish color of dead
> *vegetarian*.
> (*Vegetation*.)

Other examples are *climatic* for *climactic, statue* for *stature* (or vice versa), *incidences* for *incidents,* and *course* for *coarse.*

Non-words should never be used: for example, *interpretate* for *interpret* and *predominately* for *predominantly.*

Exercise 2

VOCABULARY TEST—*One of the best ways to gain exactness in your writing is to expand your vocabulary.*

Be word-conscious. Watch for new words and new meanings as you read; determine the meanings of new words from context; use your dictionary. It is not helpful merely to memorize new words. A grasp of the ideas connected with a word helps to make it yours.

For each group below, put in the parentheses the number (one to five) of the word or phrase which most nearly expresses the meaning of the italicized word in the context given.[1]

1. Defending his action with *specious* reasoning (   )
   1. brilliant 2. long-winded 3. falsely plausible
   4. minutely detailed 5. outstanding
2. Much *caviling* at the new ruling announced by the school committee (   )
   1. quarreling 2. making trivial objections 3. jeering
   4. hesitating 5. getting angry
3. Protesting that he should not be censured, since his misdeeds were at most *peccadilloes* (   )
   1. differences of opinion 2. political favors 3. love affairs 4. small offenses 5. misunderstandings

---

[1]Copyright © 1968 by G. & C. Merriam Company. Reprinted by permission.

4. Northerners find that country's climate very *enervating*. ( )
   1. weakening 2. strengthening 3. annoying
   4. pleasant 5. bracing
5. Slipping out at night to *clandestine* meetings ( )
   1. infrequent 2. important 3. happy 4. secret
   5. forbidden
6. Much given to using *pejorative* epithets ( )
   1. scandalous 2. obscene 3. ineffective
   4. exaggerated 5. disparaging
7. Urged to *emulate* his older brother ( )
   1. imitate 2. ridicule 3. sacrifice 4. praise
   5. admire
8. A very rich man surrounded by *sycophants* ( )
   1. cronies 2. flatterers 3. sensualists
   4. mind readers 5. quack doctors
9. Heaven as a place of *ineffable* joys ( )
   1. unlikely 2. indescribable 3. unearthly
   4. impossible 5. ineradicable
10. A policy that the government has never fully *elucidated* ( )
    1. explained 2. carried out 3. escaped
    4. made smooth 5. decided
11. Often teased about his *propensity* for having his picture taken ( )
    1. reason 2. inclination 3. skill 4. dislike
    5. ability
12. What he wanted was a soft job with a *munificent* salary. ( )
    1. reasonable 2. modest 3. very generous 4. paid
    in advance 5. deferred

13. A *plethora* of different models and styles of automobiles (   )
    1. great number 2. majority 3. sufficiency
    4. excess 5. deficiency
14. A *laconic* telegram telling him to come home (   )
    1. cynical 2. of few words 3. bitter 4. special
    5. amusing
15. Advertising and promotion cost an *unconscionable* sum. (   )
    1. impossible 2. uncertain 3. modest 4. sizable
    5. unreasonable
16. A *fortuitous* meeting that had fateful consequences (   )
    1. secret 2. difficult 3. successful 4. scheduled
    5. accidental
17. Advice from an expert to a *tyro* (   )
    1. spinner 2. beginner 3. bandit 4. foreigner
    5. business leader
18. Asking his doctor for an *analgesic* drug (   )
    1. hallucinating 2. habit-forming 3. poisonous
    4. pain-killing 5. innocuous
19. The more *callow* observers still insist that the organization is a tool of Western diplomacy. (   )
    1. unsophisticated 2. stupid 3. youthful
    4. shrewd 5. experienced
20. *Sardonic* laughter of satirists (   )
    1. brief 2. gay 3. mocking 4. absurd
    5. unwelcome
21. Platitudinous, *jejune* lectures (   )
    1. trivial 2. uninteresting 3. amateurish 4. novel
    5. exciting

22. People that *scouted* the idea of the airplane's being of any practical value ( )

1. considered 2. advocated 3. urged 4. accepted eagerly 5. rejected scornfully

23. Expecting his parents to *demur* at his having a car ( )

1. speak soothingly 2. become enraged 3. object 4. agree 5. reply

24. Making a *precarious* living as a free-lance writer ( )

1. uncertain 2. modest 3. good 4. comfortable 5. desirable.

25. His friends were most *sanguine* about his chance of winning. ( )

1. worried 2. sad 3. pessimistic 4. optimistic 5. pleased

26. A method that *obviates* the need for special tools ( )

1. makes clear 2. makes easy 3. requires 4. turns aside 5. makes unnecessary

27. Forced to *recant* all opinions differing from the leadership ( )

1. silence 2. denounce 3. renounce 4. applaud 5. repeat

28. *Exhilarated* by the warm sun and the fresh breeze ( )

1. made apprehensive 2. stimulated 3. tired out 4. destroyed 5. heartened

29. *Inveterate* opponents of government policy ( )

1. very old 2. habitual 3. feminine 4. expert 5. retired

30. *Aprocryphal* stories like that of Washington and the cherry tree (   )
    1. traditional   2. visionary   3. not flattering
    4. not authentic   5. prophetic
31. The doctor's *prognosis* was discouraging. (   )
    1. disease   2. treatment   3. prediction   4. analysis
    5. attitude
32. Statements that were not actually lies, but rather *disingenuous* half-truths (   )
    1. not candid   2. not clever   3. credulous
    4. unfavorable   5. not real
33. The clichés of anti-Communist *polemics* (   )
    1. orations   2. political activities   3. theories
    4. controversial arguments   5. religious beliefs
34. Ruthlessly *arrogating* to himself legislative and judicial powers of the state (   )
    1. desiring   2. usurping   3. pleading   4. demanding
    5. abandoning
35. Broadly sympathetic and understanding, but *extenuates* nothing nor makes the bad appear good (   )
    1. makes excuses for   2. explains in detail
    3. condemns   4. holds back   5. covers up
36. A *practicable* method of desalting seawater (   )
    1. much used   2. ordinary   3. feasible
    4. not theoretical   5. possible
37. Jeered at in the streets by children and *harridans* (   )
    1. distance runners   2. drunkards
    3. peace marchers   4. scolding old women
    5. grouchy old men
38. Taut nerves and *flaccid* muscles (   )
    1. bulging   2. limp   3. exhausted   4. sound
    5. strained

39. The *gratuitous* assumption that men work only for money ( )
    1. thankful 2. generous 3. graceful
    4. well-deserved 5. uncalled-for
40. His judgment is faulty but his honesty has never been *impugned.* ( )
    1. destroyed 2. criticized 3. attacked with words
    4. discredited 5. doubted
41. An act of selfless generosity that will *redound* to his credit ( )
    1. become added 2. echo 3. reestablish 4. become useless 5. make a noise
42. A bold, original thinker, not *amenable* to group pressures ( )
    1. pleasant 2. suitable 3. tractable 4. necessary
    5. desirable
43. A speech marred by frequent *solecisms* ( )
    1. blunders 2. witty remarks 3. conceits 4. puns
    5. stolen ideas
44. *Querulous* voices of tired children ( )
    1. hostile 2. belligerent 3. threatening
    4. complaining 5. questioning.
45. A judge famous for *excoriating* perjured witnesses ( )
    1. sympathizing with 2. censuring scathingly
    3. torturing 4. annoying 5. detesting
46. The literary influence of the Twenties is becoming increasingly *attenuated.* ( )
    1. ignored 2. enlarged 3. paid attention to
    4. weakened 5. made clear
47. Extremely *dilatory* in answering letters ( )
    1. delaying 2. wordy 3. pleasing 4. prompt
    5. expansive

48. Anxious to display his knowledge of a *recondite* subject ( )
    1. peculiar   2. forgotten   3. sacred   4. obscure
    5. foreign
49. The *enigmatic* foreign policy of our ally   ( )
    1. suspicious   2. unpleasant   3. puzzling   4. difficult
    5. unlikely
50. *Forensic* eloquence of a trial lawyer   ( )
    1. unusual   2. brilliant   3. rhetorical   4. powerful
    5. dramatic

Exercise 3

In each of the following passages select from the alternatives in parentheses the word or phrase which you think the author used. The choices involve exactness in meaning, idiom, triteness or originality, level of diction, and just plain good taste. If more than one choice is acceptable, base your decision on the choice of words and phrases in the rest of the passage. Be prepared to defend your selections.

1

Karl Marx was born in Trier, Germany, the (offspring, son, progeny) of a lawyer. He was educated at the Universities of Bonn and Berlin and was (granted, given, favored with) the Ph.D. degree in 1842. Marx had first (craved, opted for, hoped for) a university (job, career, vocation), but his (radical, extreme, far out) views made this difficult. He began work on a radical newspaper in Germany, and (ere long, anon, soon) became one of its editors. However, within a year the newspaper was (suppressed, quelled, squelched), and Marx left for Paris —

then (a center of, the most in, the middle of) socialist thought. He met Friedrich Engels there. In 1848 they (whipped out, issued, coevally consummated) the *Communist Manifesto* pamphlet. At about this time Marx was (banned from, kicked out of, excommunicated from) Germany; he was, moreover, told by French (bigwigs, authorities, powers) that in that country he could (exist, live, domicile) only in a (wee, small, infinitesimal) provincial community; hence he decided to move on to London where he (dwelt, remained, abided) for the rest of his life. He wrote *The Critique of Political Economy* in 1859, and Volume I of *Das Kapital* in 1867. He (died, succumbed, passed away) in 1883 without completing the remainder of *Das Kapital*.

FRANCIS R. ALLEN, *Socio-cultural Dynamics:*
An Introduction to Social Change

2

The following is the "Statement of Purpose" from the Catalog *of Yankton College, Yankton, South Dakota.*

The central purpose of Yankton College is to provide a setting in which young (ladies and gentlemen, boys and girls, men and women) can make (significant, great, fantastic) progress toward becoming (older, mature, developed) and fully functioning adults in (a chaotic, an enigmatic, a complex) world. Such a goal is (ostensibly, apparently, obviously) a task for a lifetime of (asking questions, inquiring, wondering), but the four years at Yankton College constitute (an effective, a good, a wonderful) commencement.

To realize this ideal, Yankton College is committed to (tender, offer) the (nicest, best, most superb) possible liberal arts education in a (place, setting, space) which permits the individual as much (independence, unrestraint, permissiveness) in his study as his own capabilities allow. We believe that to become (smart, bright, educated) the student should be exposed to each of the (stupendous, fine, great) areas of knowledge: the humanities, the social sciences, the natural sciences and the performing and fine arts. In keeping with the (tradition, custom, mores) of the liberal arts, our (intention, battleplan, notion) is to provide the student with a curriculum of such nature as to (implant, instill, imbue) in him the desire to (engage, fight, veto) ignorance, prejudice, and parochialism in our society.

3

The following is a description by a modern biographer of life in a Russian prison as it was experienced by the novelist Feodor Dostoevsky in the nineteenth century.

Life in prison was life still. It asserted itself in this bleak place like grass (growing, thrusting its way) between slabs of granite. The brutal severity of the regimen was to some degree mitigated (for, by, with) incredible laxity. The (convicts, jailbirds, criminals) were not permitted to do any work for themselves to earn money. Nevertheless, as soon as the doors were locked for the night the barracks would turn into a humming workshop. Many pursued (a hobby, a craft, an art), some engaged in buying and selling and in financial transactions of sorts, and there were those who hired themselves out to their mates as entertainers, lookout men, (factotums, stooges, cronies). All managed to earn something and were able to secure certain (amenities, goodies, luxuries). Some ate other than prison food. Cards, (nicotine, tobacco, pot), vodka were strictly (forbidden, taboo), yet gambling, smoking, and drinking thrived, and the more enterprising even got themselves (ladies, broads, women) by (bribing, greasing the palms of) the guards. Money was precious as a symbol of freedom, the dream even of "lifers." Yet they used it in the most spendthrift fashion, fearing that it would be (violently requisitioned, purloined, snatched) from them before they could enjoy it, and also in order to secure the respect of their fellows by a splurge. Of course, all infringements of discipline were committed at the peril of reprisals. Eight Eyes would descend like the wolf on the fold, goods and money would be confiscated, and the offenders (flogged, flagellated, chastised).

Only Christmas and Easter were days of (amusement, leisure, revelry), and on these occasions relaxation of discipline was, if not sanctioned, at least connived at. New Year's Eve (in the year of 1852, somewhere around 1852, 1852) was marked by a unique event: the convicts, under Dostoevsky's (direction, bossing, tyranny), staged a comedy, a farce, and a musical pantomime. The (spectacular, happening, spectacle) was attended not only by the inmates but also by the prison officials and other (big shots, "noble and highborn persons," VIPs), for whose benefit a playbill was posted. There were no theatricals in the city and the show was a huge success.

AVRAHM YARMOLINSKY, Dostoevsky: Works and Days

4

Shakespeare, who thought (a lot, a great deal, a whole lot) about the relations of fathers and children, makes this problem the subject of several of his (best, fine) plays. He shows us a father who, with vast dexterity and (push, ginger, vinegar, energy), has won himself a (good job, great position). The (dad, forebear, father) loves his (boy, progeny, son), and hopes that he will share the (loot, rewards, prizes) and (privileges, responsibilities, love) of power. The (kid, brat, son, boy) is (keen, talented, smart) and (cute, charming, sweet), brave and (peppy, energetic, pushy). It would be (easy, a push-over), one would think, and (fun, pleasant) for him to (throw in with, amalgamate with, join) his (sire, old man, father). (There's, There is) no compulsion. He can do (as he liketh, whatever he likes). He may sit at home playing shove-ha'penny if he (selects, wants to, chooses); or hunt all week during the season; or (diddle around, waste time harmlessly) in other ways. But he chooses to become a (mobster, gangster). He is only an amateur, but he is on the fringe of the (pro, professional) crooks. His best (chum, friend, pal) is a broken-down old (villain, ruffian, codger) who has drunk (most, almost) all his gifts (away, down, up) and is living (by, off, on) the (balance, remainder) of his (head, mind, wits). He (sees far more of, runs around more with) Falstaff than he does (of, with) his father, King Henry IV. He makes Falstaff into a (sort of, sort of a) (substitute, second-string, sub) father, (carrying on, laughing) with him as he (can't, cannot) with his father, tricking and (joshing, befooling) him as he would like to (belittle, run down) his father. As the play goes on, it is (harder and harder, tougher and tougher) to understand (what's, what is) wrong with Hal. Why should he throw away his chances? Why does he want to hurt his father? He *says* he is doing it (so, so that) he can get more praise for reforming later; but that is not the real (answer, reason), and it never comes up after his (reform, going straight) takes place. The real reason (appears, shows up) when his father is in genuine danger and when Hal himself is challenged by a rival of his own age. Then he rushes to help the king's cause, and kills his challenger, Hotspur.

GILBERT HIGHET, *The Art of Teaching*

5

One of the reasons that country (folks, hicks, folk), with limited experience, are nevertheless so much better (pals, companions, associates) for (an artist, a longhair, an artiste) or a (Ph.D., thinker, brain) than city (slicks, people) of the same (class, category), is that the former have always kept for themselves a little free time to sit still and (breed, cogitate, brood), whittling wood around a winter fire, or bent impassively over a fishing pole, watching the trout's (canny, sharp, smart) (movements, flirtations, cavortings). The city worker (maybe, may be) better read; but the countryman is more (intelligent, intellectual, reflective): such experience as he has (experienced, encountered, met) he has (saved, salted down, preserved).

LEWIS MUMFORD, *Faith for Living*

6

When one considers (American, U.S.) history (as, on) a whole, it is hard to think of any very long period in which it could be said that the country has been (constantly, consistently) well (run, governed). And yet its political (scheme, system) is, on (a, the) whole, a resilient and well-seasoned one, and on the strength of its history one must (assume, presume) that it can summon enough talent and good will to cope with its (afflictions, ills).

RICHARD HOFSTADTER, "Reflections on Violence in the United States"

38 Wordiness *W*

Avoid redundancy.

Omit needless words and irrelevant ideas. Conciseness increases the force of writing.

> Accidents due to excessive speed often end fatally for those involved. (11 words)
>
> Accidents due to excessive speed often end fatally. (8 words)

Use one word for many.

> The love letter was written by somebody who did not sign his name. (13 words)
>
> The love letter was anonymous (*or*, was not signed). (5 or 6 words)

Use the active voice for conciseness. (See §5.)

> The truck was overloaded by the workmen. (7 words)
> The workmen overloaded the truck. (5 words)

Revise sentence structure for conciseness.

> Another element which adds to the effectiveness of a speech is its emotional content. (14 words)
>
> Emotional content also makes a speech more effective. (8 words)

Use one word, not two with the same meaning (tautology).

> Basic and fundamental principles. (4 words)
> Basic principles. (2 words)

Study your sentences carefully and make them concise by using all the methods discussed above.

However, do not sacrifice concreteness and vividness for conciseness and brevity.

CONCRETE
AND VIVID

At each end of the sunken garden, worn granite steps, flanked by large magnolia trees, lead to the formal paths.

EXCESSIVELY
CONCISE

The garden has steps at both ends.

Exercise 4

Express the following sentences succinctly. Do not omit important ideas.

1. The custom which has always been so popular in the country of waving to strangers as you pass them is gradually fading out.

2. There are several reasons why officers of the law ought to be trained in the law of the land, and two of these are as follows. The first of these reasons is that policemen can enforce the law better if they are familiar with it. And second, they will be less likely to violate the rights of private citizens if they know exactly and accurately what these rights are.

3. Although the Kentucky rifle played an important and significant part in getting food for the frontiersmen who settled the American West, its function as a means of protection was in no degree any less significant in their lives.

4. Some television programs assume a low level of public intelligence and present their shows to the public as if the audience were made up of morons.

5. The distant explosion was audible to the ear.

6. The Japanese beetle is a beetle which was introduced into America from Japan and which thrives on fruits and roots of grass.

7. In modern warfare every nation which is engaged in the war broadcasts over the radio information which is intended to convince the people in the enemy country that their cause is wrong.

8. It is not true that he is guilty.

9. It is a pleasure for some to indulge in eating large quantities of food at meals, but doctors of medicine tell us that such pleasures can only bring with them unpleasant results in the long run of things.

10. The essay consist of facts which describe vividly many of the events in the life of a typical juggler. In this description the author uses a vocabulary which is

easy to understand. This vocabulary is on neither too high a level nor too low a level, but on one which can be understood by any high school graduate.

39 Repetition *rep*

Avoid careless repetition of words, phrases, and sounds. Repeat only for emphasis or clarity.

Unintentional repetition is seldom effective. Avoid repetition by (1) using synonyms, (2) using pronouns, and (3) condensing sentences and omitting words.

REPETITIOUS   Consideration of others is really the main *quality* of a gentleman. This *quality* comes from the heart.

CONDENSED   Consideration of others, which is really the main quality of a gentleman, comes from the heart.

39a Do not use vague or awkward synonyms to avoid repetition.

When several synonyms are used within a few sentences, the passage usually needs condensation.

EXCESSIVE SYNONYMS   *Consideration* of others is really the main *quality* of a *gentleman*. A *man* who has this *trait* is sincere.

CONDENSED   Sincere consideration of others is really the main quality of a gentleman.

39b Avoid unpleasant repetition of sounds.

Devices like rhyme, meter, and repetition of consonant and vowel sounds are a vital part of poetry and of some kinds of creative prose, but they are generally to be avoided in expository writing.

RHYME

The biologist again *checked* his charts to determine the *effect* of the poison on the *insect*.

CORRECTION

The biologist again studied his charts to determine the effect of the poison on the moth.

REPETITION OF CONSONANTS

The *des*pe*r*ate *dep*ression of that *d*ecade *d*oomed many men.

CORRECTION

The great depression of the thirties ruined many people.

39c Repeat a word or a phrase for emphasis or for clarity.

Purposeful repetition of a word or a phrase often gains emphasis. In the following passage, the italicized words show how President Kennedy used repetition effectively.

> The world is very different now. For *man* holds in his mortal hands the power to abolish *all forms* of *human* poverty and *all forms* of *human* life. And yet the same revolutionary *beliefs* for which our forebears fought are still at issue around the globe—the *belief* that the rights of *man* come not from the generosity of the state but from the hand of God. . . .
>
> Let every nation know, whether it wishes us well or ill, that we shall pay *any* price, bear *any* burden, meet *any* hardship, support *any* friend, oppose *any* foe, in order to assure the survival and the success of liberty.
>
> JOHN F. KENNEDY, "Inaugural Address"

Besides repeated words, the passage makes effective use of repeated or parallel structures and sounds (*from . . . from* in the first paragraph; *well or ill, survival and success* in the second).

Exercise 5

Rewrite the following passage. Avoid wordiness and undesirable repetition.

A large number of people enjoy reading murder mysteries regularly. These people are not themselves murderers as a rule, nor would these people really ever enjoy seeing someone commit an actual murder, nor would most of them actually enjoy trying to solve an actual murder. They probably enjoy reading murder mysteries because of this reason: they have found a way to escape from the monotonous, boring routine of dull everyday existence.

To such people the murder mystery is realistic fantasy. It is realistic because the people in the murder mystery are as a general rule believable as people. They are not just made up pasteboard figures. It is also realistic because the character who is the hero, the character who solves the murder mystery, solves it not usually by trial and error and haphazard methods but by exercising a high degree of logic and reason. It is absolutely and totally essential that people who enjoy murder mysteries have an admiration for the human faculty of logic.

But murder mysteries are also fantasies. The people who read such books of fiction play a game. It is a game in which they suspend certain human emotions. One of these human emotions that they suspend is pity. If the reader stops to feel pity and sympathy for each and every victim that is killed or if the reader stops to feel terrible horror that such a thing could happen in our world of today, he will never enjoy reading murder mysteries. The devoted reader of murder mysteries keeps uppermost in his mind always and at all times the goal of arriving through logic and observation at the final solution to the mystery offered to him in the book. It is a game with life and death. Whodunits hopefully help him or her to hide from the hideous horrors of actual life and death in the real world.

40 Vagueness—Specific and Concrete Words *vag*

Do not write vaguely. Choose words that are as specific and as concrete as your meaning requires.

Avoid sentences which can have many different meanings.

The weather was undesirable.

The sentence above could mean several things:

Heavy rains caused a flash flood.
The baseball game was rained out.
During the long drought all the crops failed except the peanuts.

Writing which is too unspecific to convey a clear meaning can cause misunderstanding. *To abstract* means "to draw from"—in particular, to draw general concepts from specific instances. The diagram below is a simple illustration; each step to the right represents a further abstraction.

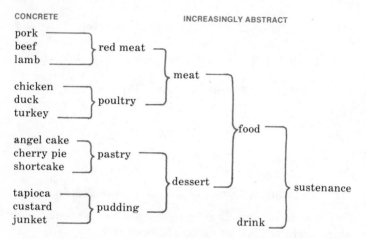

CONCRETE   INCREASINGLY ABSTRACT

Without the power to abstract, we would be bound to the immediate object or experience. We could never talk about "a meal," but only "roast beef and baked potato." Increasingly abstract concepts like *meat, food, meal,* and *sustenance* allow us to group large numbers of objects, ideas, and experiences and to combine abstractions in order to discover still more relationships — in short, to think.

Abstractions like *food, drink,* and *sustenance* derive from concrete experience common to all. But we do not independently arrive at all the abstractions we use. Rather, we borrow most of them ready-made. Consider a few high-level abstractions like *integrity, morality, freedom, goodness, love, justice, democracy.*

Love means something a little different to almost everyone who uses the word. Many abstractions (*democracy* and *liberty*, for example) are not simple sums of concrete facts; instead, they are built on such a complex of other abstractions that it is hard to say just what they mean. Because such words are hard to define and because they may mean many things, one should always know what he means when he uses them.

Notice how the following passage improves as it becomes more specific and concrete.

GENERAL

Mankind needs to recognize the geographical limitations of communities and the advantages of changes in environment. This is a principle which is evident in the movements and migrations of the creatures of nature.

MORE SPECIFIC

For the improvement of one's health, a change of environment is advisable. It is fortunate that no one place encompasses the world. The vegetation and birds of one place do not exist in another. Migratory birds are more cosmopolitan than man; they eat their meals each day in a different part of the country. Even some animals follow the seasons.

VERY SPECIFIC

To the sick the doctors wisely recommend a change of air and scenery. Thank Heaven, here is not all the world. The buckeye does not grow in New England, and the mockingbird is rarely heard here. The wild goose is more of a cosmopolite than we; he breaks his fast in Canada, takes a luncheon in the Ohio, and plumes himself for the night in a southern bayou. Even the bison, to some extent, keeps pace with the seasons, cropping the pastures of the Colorado only till a greener and sweeter grass awaits him by the Yellowstone.

HENRY DAVID THOREAU, *Walden*

Exercise 6

Change words and details in the following sentences so that they become exact, concrete, specific.

1. He consumed the food.
2. She went across the street.
3. The sunset was colorful.
4. The vegetation was thick.
5. The furniture was damaged.

Exercise 7

Write your personal definition of one of the following abstract terms in a paragraph of about two hundred words. Give concrete examples from your experience.

> virtue   courage   imagination   humor

41 Connotation *con*

Choose words with connotations appropriate to tone and content.

In addition to dictionary or denotative meanings, many words carry special associations or suggestions, known as **connotations.** The **denotation** of a word is its precise meaning, the exact definition given in a dictionary. Denotatively, a dog is a four-legged carnivorous domesticated mammal. Literally viewed in its denotative meaning (if that is possible), the word *dog* arouses no emotional response of any kind, no hatred, no affection.

Connotations include emotional responses. What *dog* suggests to the reader or writer in addition to *four-legged carnivore* is the word's connotation, which can be pleasant or unpleasant. To one person the word *dog* may suggest friendship; to another once attacked by a dog the word may connote terror.

A good writer uses connotations and evokes planned emotional reactions to particular words. To suggest the sophisticated, he may mention a *lap dog;* to evoke the amusing or the rural, he may use *hound dog.* To connote a social or moral distinction, he may call someone a *cur.* Even this word may have different connotations: a social worker may react sympathetically to it; a snob, contemptuously. Consider the associations aroused by other words naming dogs: *canine, pooch, mutt, mongrel, puppy,* and *watchdog.* Even some breeds of dog arouse different responses: *bloodhound, shepherd, St. Bernard, poodle.*

Words that are denotative synonyms may have very different connotative overtones. Consider the following:

    janitor – custodian – building superintendent
    drummer – salesman – field representative
    slender – thin – skinny
    resolute – strong-willed – stubborn

The tactful writer avoids a word with unpleasant connotations and chooses a synonym which connotes greater status or respect. Yet false elegance can also create unpleasant connotations.

Be sure that the words you choose give the suggestions you wish to convey. A single word with the wrong connotation can easily spoil a passage. Only one word has been changed in the following quotation:

Let us never dicker out of fear. But let us never fear to dicker.

President Kennedy actually wrote:

> Let us never negotiate out of fear. But let us never fear to negotiate.

The word *dicker* would ruin the tone of the statement even though it is a fairly close synonym for *negotiate*.

Exercise 8

Words which have approximately the same denotation frequently suggest responses that are quite different. The combinations below bring together words with different connotations. Rate each word for favorability of connotation, 1 for most favorable, 2 for second, 3 for least. Be prepared to defend your decisions and to explain the different shades of connotation.

1. diseased
   ill
   sick

2. fat
   overweight
   stout

3. economical
   stingy
   thrifty

4. controlled substance
   drug
   narcotic

5. decay
   decompose
   rot

6. harsh
   severe
   stern

7. languish
   shrivel
   wither

8. enthusiast
   extremist
   fanatic

9. garbage
   rubbish
   trash

10. impractical
    quixotic
    romantic

11. little
    petite
    small

12. innocent
    naïve
    simple

13. impulsive
    spontaneous
    unconstrained

14. famous
    notorious
    well-known

15. aging
    mature
    mellow

42 Figurative Language *fig*

Use fresh, imaginative, and appropriate figures of speech. Avoid mixed figures.

Do not assume (1) that college writing need be drab or solemn, or (2) that to be figurative you must be flowery or pretentious.

42a Use figurative comparisons.

Learn to observe and compare things. Describe abstractions in concrete and human terms. Personify.

the voice of history
the welcoming, embracing night

Write metaphors, implied comparisons.

The kitten is a tiny ball of fuzz.
Historians constantly stir the ashes of the past.
The mind is a house of many mirrors.

Write similes, comparisons stated with *like* or *as*.

> Life is sometimes like a circus.
> The mind is like a house of many mirrors.
> The crowds of people ran about like frightened ants.

Listen for figures of speech in conversation and watch for them in things you read. Try to use them in your own speech and writing. Study the following figures from Eudora Welty's "Old Mr. Marblehall."

> A voice "dizzies other ladies like an organ note, and amuses men like a halloo down the well."
>
> Drapes are "as tall as the wicked queens in Italian tales."
>
> An old man in an overcoat is "as gratified as an animal in its own tingling fur."
>
> A fat woman "rolls back into the house as if she had been on a little wheel all this time."

As you develop the habit of observing and comparing things, good figures of speech will begin to come to you naturally, particularly when they help you describe or characterize something in a vivid word or two. Avoid stock figures that have long been worn out.

42b Avoid strained, mixed, or inappropriate figures of speech.

A mixed figure is a blend of several images, usually incongruous or absurd. It is corrected by being made consistent.

ABSURD The United States is following in the same steps that the Roman Empire took toward its downfall. These steps are eating away at the very heart of our society—the younger generation.

CONSISTENT The United States is following the same road that the Roman Empire took toward its downfall. This road will lead to the ruin of our younger generation.

CONFUSED When put to the acid test, his principles were found to be as crazy as a loon.

CONSISTENT When put to the acid test, his principles dissolved.

43 Fine Writing *fw*

Avoid flowery language.

Fine writing is ornate, falsely poetic language which is often pompous and artificial. *These United States* rather than *the United States*, *in the year of 1976* rather than *in 1976*, *at this point in time* rather than *now*, for example, have the ring of affectation. *Green lawn*—or even *lawn*—is more natural than *verdant sward*. *Spade or shovel* is more natural than *simple instrument for delving into Mother Earth.*

FINE WRITING The competitor in the pigskin sport suffered from a poignant affliction.

NATURAL The football player had a sprained ankle.

FINE WRITING As a young lad I delighted in laving my feet in the purling stream which flowed behind our domicile.

NATURAL As a boy I enjoyed wading in the creek behind our house.

FINE WRITING He stretched his limbs on the downy couch just as Old Sol first shone in all his glory through the leafy foliage.

NATURAL He went to bed at dawn.

The Process of Composition

Good writing is thoughtfully planned and carefully developed, whether it be in a single paragraph or a long paper based on special reading. Sections 44 to 48 offer guidelines for the composition process as a whole, for the kind of thinking which underlies good writing, for clear and orderly paragraphing, for themes on general subjects and on literary topics, and for the long paper based on special investigation.

44 Clear and Logical Thinking *log*

Good factual writing must be accurate and sufficiently informed. Errors of fact shake your reader's confidence in you if he detects them; they misinform and mislead him if he does not. Good argument must be clear and logical. Faulty logic may give rise to serious misunderstandings even when both writer and reader have the best intentions.

44a **Use only accurate and verified data.**

Facts, which are demonstrable, are different from judgment, which is based on facts. A reader who does not have specific information should refrain from making a judgment. It is best to distinguish clearly between facts and the conclusions reached from them and to explain clearly how judgments derive from facts.

Errors of fact, committed through carelessness, ignorance, or dishonesty, lead to distrust and doubt. If the reader can disprove one thing which is stated as a fact, he will be likely to doubt the accuracy of a conclusion based on it. Further, he will be suspicious of other statements presented as facts.

The following statements are immediately suspect because of errors of fact:

1. Shakespeare's language seems old-fashioned to us because he lived in the Middle Ages. (Shakespeare lived in the Renaissance, long after the Middle Ages.)

2. Arthur Wegelin testified that he had entered the country on June 31, 1973. (Thirty days hath June.)

3. Only wealthy people buy original oil paintings. (The facts will not bear out this contention.)

44b **Use reliable authority.**

Authorities often disagree with each other. Then it becomes a writer's responsibility to weigh their opinions against each other and if possible to choose. When you cannot yourself reach a sound decision, certain criteria can tell you some things about the reliability of opinions.

1. What is the reputation of the writer or the work in the given field? The opinions of other writers on the subject, the comments in annotated bibliographies, and, for more recent works, the critical reviews which you can find by using the *Book Review Digest* will give you some basis for judgment.

2. Is the writer a specialist on *this* subject? A competent specialist in one field may not be an authority in other fields. A scientist whose word on nuclear energy is definitive is not necessarily an authority on foreign affairs. A sports writer who can be cited with confidence on the history of the World Series may be highly unreliable on the history of art.

3. How objective is the source? If it strikes you as prejudiced or one-sided, check it against the facts and against the works of other authorities. Two biographies of the same man may give two very different pictures of him.

4. How exactly and to what extent does an authority admit to the complexity of an issue and describe his own uncertainties? Sometimes the more reliable source takes a less positive stand than an erroneous extremist who seems to know the exact truth.

5. Does the writer distinguish fact from opinion? An opinion should be presented as such and not stated as though it were a fact.

6. Does the source give you the latest significant information? Sometimes the information of an earlier source is superseded by later findings. Consider the date of publication.

44c Avoid sweeping generalizations.

Even when the facts are accurate, they may be numerically insufficient to support a generalization. If you know that three of your friends oppose capital punishment, you should not leap to the conclusion that "Everyone wishes to have capital punishment abolished." The statement is too broad for the evidence on which it is based. Generalizations like the following may contain some elements of truth, but they claim far too much:

> The very rich avoid paying income taxes.
> College professors have no real concern for their students.
> A businessman is not interested in the arts.
> Germanic people do not have a sense of humor.
> Mediterranean people are hot-tempered.

Sweeping statements about nationalities and races, of course, have been some of the most illogical and pernicious arguments of history. Generalizations about professions, social and economic groups and classes are widely prevalent; but often they contain inaccuracies because they include too many people and because the descriptions or statements are too extreme. You can reach a sound generalization about a group of persons or things only after you have examined enough of them to know that many or all of them share the condition or situation which you are describing.

44d Use enough specific evidence.

If conclusions are not based upon sufficient information, the content of an entire paper may be questionable. The true scholar grounds his conclusions on sufficient data arrived at through careful study of the findings of others and through his own painstaking research. In the same way, the writer of an expository paper should accumulate and present enough evidence to justify the point he is making.

44e Stick to the point.

Do not introduce irrelevancies or wander off the subject. First paragraphs of papers are sometimes especially irrelevant because they begin at a point too far removed from the main subject. Digression is a sign of inability to focus attention on the problem at hand.

44f Do not ignore conflicting facts or evidence.

Be aware of facts and instances which seem to refute your own views and conclusions, and be prepared to deal with them. You can actually strengthen your case by taking opposing evidence into consideration and showing why it is insignificant, irrelevant, or exceptional.

44g Do not beg the question or reason in a circle.

A writer begs the question when he assumes that something is true and writes as if he had proved it. Here is an example:

> A large part of the taxpayer's educational dollar is spent on unnecessary items like school lunchrooms, classes for handicapped children, and instruction in art and music.

That the educational items mentioned are "unnecessary" ones is a debatable proposition which the writer does not establish but merely asserts. Suppose he defends it, when challenged, as follows:

> These items are unnecessary because they are "extras," and "extras" are things that are not needed.

He is still begging the question (arguing in a circle) because he is simply restating the proposition in terms of itself.

44h Do not omit essential steps in the thought or draw false conclusions from unstated assumptions.

The omission of basic details in a train of thought may leave the reader puzzled or confused. Some elementary steps may be skipped when a specialist is writing for specialists; but the more general the audience, the fewer the steps that may be omitted. The problem here is one of clarity rather than logic.

A logical fallacy, however, results whenever the omission of a step in the reasoning leads to a false conclusion. If one argues, for example, that "He cannot be elected to Phi Beta Kappa because he is a football player," the argument is based on a false assumption: that no football player ever makes good grades, or that Phi Beta Kappa will refuse to elect someone who plays football. Similar omissions of parts of the argument occur in the following sentences. What are the unstated assumptions, and why are the conclusions false?

> Since he made good grades in high school, he will undoubtedly be a good student in college.
>
> He will not make a good judge because he was once fined for speeding.

He has a wonderful personality and will certainly be successful as a salesman.

44i Do not substitute an appeal to emotions for an appeal to reason.

Emotional appeal has its proper place, but it should never
be substituted for logical thinking.

Name-calling is an appeal to prejudice. Do not becloud
an issue by calling an opponent a moron. This is argument against a man rather than against a principle or a
point of view.

"Loaded" words attempt to shape an attitude through
prejudice instead of reason. In loaded terms a government subsidy plan might become a "hand-out scheme that
a bunch of radical do-gooders are trying to fasten on the
taxpayers."

Flattery attempts to persuade through excessive
praise. The political candidate who tells an audience that
he knows they will vote for him because of their high intelligence is attempting to convince by flattering.

Snob appeal asserts that one should adopt a certain
view because all the better people do — including, of
course, the writer. "More corporation presidents smoke El
Ropo than any other cigar" is a favorite form of fallacious
advertising.

Mass appeal attempts to persuade by asserting that
everyone follows the pattern favored by the writer. It
suggests that one is in error if he does not follow the
herd: everyone ought to go to college; everyone ought to
own his home.

44j **Do not draw unwarranted conclusions about cause and effect.**

When two things happen in sequence, the second is not necessarily caused by the first. If a man walks under a ladder and shortly thereafter loses his wallet, he is not justified in assuming that he lost his wallet *because* he walked under the ladder. To show a cause-and-effect relationship between two events, it is necessary to produce evidence in addition to the mere fact that one preceded the other. Otherwise we would have to conclude that 1969 caused 1970.

44k **Express ideas with moderation.**

Be temperate in your judgments and in your choice of words. Overstatement, overemphasis, and dogmatic assertion not only irritate most readers but arouse doubt or even disbelief. The good writer knows better than to be cocksure and brash. He is careful to state that something "usually" happens in a particular situation, that a given result occurs "in most cases," and that an outcome will "probably" be a happy one or "perhaps" a disastrous one. On the other hand, when dealing with certainty, be certain.

44L **Allow for adequate alternatives.**

On some questions it is faulty logic to assume that there are *two and only two* alternatives. Often a number of possibilities exist. If, for example, a father tells his son that he must go to college or else fail in life, he has not allowed for the possibility that the son may succeed without a college education. It is tempting, because dramatic, to present things in terms of two extremes, but a simple *either-or* proposition of this kind is not always valid.

Exercise

Describe the errors in content and thought in each of the following.

1. The fact that the lexicographer wrote the publisher about his objections to the novel proves that as fiction it was not worth publishing.

2. Most good students do very well in either English or mathematics; but only a few good students do well in both.

3. An interjection is a word or a clause used to express a strong emotion.

4. Russian medicine is far behind this country's because Russia has so many women doctors.

5. The book which you reviewed favorably is trash, the kind of dirty garbage found on the cheapest shelves of pornographic bookstores.

6. Anyone who reaches eighteen is old enough to make his own decisions without advice from other people.

7. The highest percentage that the United States government takes in income tax is eighty percent.

8. Nearly all the great monuments of this world are made of marble.

9. China is far ahead of the United States in its consideration for the rights of its people. When our emissaries go to China, there is no disorder in the streets.

10. The fact that you could espouse the cause of those rebels shows me that you are a coward and a degenerate.

11. After only one week at Reduso Spa, Mrs. Wentworth lost sixteen pounds. Enroll now if you really wish to lose weight.

12. My professor must be a good scholar; he is a member of the Modern Language Association.

13. Any young man should go to trade school before going to college because it is extremely difficult for a college graduate to get a good job unless he can do something with his hands.

14. Order our new device for restoring hair in your bald spots, and new hair will begin to grow within two weeks.

15. The only good kinds of narratives are fiction and auto-biography.

16. His parents deserted him when he was an infant. No wonder he has spent much of his life in prison.

17. The welfare system in this country makes the people who have earned their money give it away to lazy good-for-nothings who are not willing to work for themselves.

18. Our state university is one of the three greatest universities in the world.

19. Three young men from this neighborhood went to college and came home addicted to drugs; in these times a young man should not seek a higher education.

20. Freedom is a necessary ingredient in the life of every woman, and every woman should make her decisions without advice because of her need for liberation.

21. According to the high school chemistry text, the article in *Chemical Research Journal* cannot be correct.

22. Subscribe to *Now*, the intellectual's magazine, and join the most enlightened readers of the day.

23. Shakespeare did not write the plays attributed to him. This fact has been proved by a famous surgeon who recently retired from a medical career to which he had devoted almost all his energy.

24. Who says fortune tellers are fakes? Just as the palmist said, I went to Alaska three months after she told my fortune.

25. A well-written theme must be in chronological order.

45 | Writing Good Paragraphs ⁊

The typical paragraph in modern writing is a group of three to ten sentences which develop one central purpose or idea. For the writer, careful paragraphing is an aspect of accurate thinking and logical organization. For the reader, clear and orderly paragraphs help comprehension by marking thought units and giving a sense of separation and progression.

45a Express the main idea of a paragraph in a topic sentence.

Good topic sentences are a major characteristic of good writing, the main signposts that indicate where a paper is going. Usually they come at the beginnings of paragraphs, but not always. The topic sentence should indicate explicitly or indirectly the unique function of the paragraph and what its connection is to the thesis sentence of the paper. The body of the paragraph adds evidence and develops the main idea but does not control the direction of the reasoning. That is the task of topic sentences. Reading only the first sentences of paragraphs in a good composition will often indicate clearly the main points of the paper.

You can test the quality of your topic sentences and the movement of your paper as a whole by the following method. In your rough draft underline the topic sentence for each paragraph; then read these sentences in sequence to see whether your argument proceeds logically and clearly. If the lines of thought are not clear, you will need to state ideas that you had previously neglected to express. Possibly you will need to fill in gaps in your thinking and to arrive at generalizations which you had not even thought of before. Then write your second draft, let it cool a little, and apply this test again.

In the three following paragraphs, the topic sentences are italicized.

The standard Horatio Alger hero was a fatherless boy of fifteen or thereabouts who had to earn his way, usually in New York City. Sometimes he had to help support a widowed mother with his boot-blacking or peddling; sometimes his parentage was unknown and he lived with an aged and eccentric miser, or with a strange hermit who claimed to be his uncle. It might even be that his father was living, but was having trouble with the mortgage on the old farm. Always, however, the boy had to stand on his own feet and face the practical problem of getting on.

This problem was set before the reader in exact financial detail. On the very first page of *Do and Dare*, for example, it was disclosed that the young hero's mother, as postmistress at Wayneboro, had made during the preceding year just $398.50. Whenever "our hero" had to deal with a mortgage, the reader was told the precise amount, the rate of interest, and all other details. When our hero took a job, the reader could figure for himself exactly how much progress he was making by getting $5 a week in wages at the jewelry store and another $5 a week tutoring Mrs. Mason's son in Latin. Our hero was always a good boy, honest, abstemious (in fact, sometimes unduly disposed to preach to drinkers and smokers), prudent, well mannered (except perhaps for the preaching), and frugal. The excitement of each book lay in his progress toward wealth.

Always there were villains who stood in his way—crooks who would rob him of his earnings, sharpers who would prey upon his supposed innocence. His battles with these villains furnished plenty of melodrama. They tried to sell him worthless gold watches on railroad trains, held him up as he was buggy-driving home with his employer's funds, kidnaped him and held him a prisoner in a New York hide-out, chloroformed him in a Philadelphia hotel room, slugged him in a Chicago alley-tenement. *But always he overcame them—with the aid of their invariable cowardice.* (There must be many men now living who remember the shock of outraged surprise with which they discovered that the village bully did not, as in the Alger books, invariably run whimpering away at the first show of manly opposition, but sometimes packed a nasty right.) The end of the book found our hero well on his way toward wealth: a fortune which might reach to more than a hundred thousand dollars, which, to the average boy reader of the seventies and eighties, was an astronomical sum. . . .

FREDERICK LEWIS ALLEN, "The Road to Riches"

Notice that the third paragraph above has a second summary sentence halfway through.

45b Write unified paragraphs. Be sure that every sentence is clearly related to the topic.

Do not wander from your point. A paragraph in which the writer is enticed off the trail by a topic other than the one he started to pursue may be described as a red-herring paragraph. In the following paragraph every detail relates to the controlling idea:

Low comedy does not balk at freaks of nature; it takes delight in them, even when they hurt. Any kind of deformity—natural or acquired—will bring the paleoridiculous running, shouting its joy at having discovered one more bit of evidence for its basic proposition: that the free spirit is yoked to a donkey and like Pinocchio may sprout long ears. Ben Turpin's crossed eyes *were* his comic talent; there was nothing else about him that was ever very funny. Bowlegs are funny, and so is Cyrano's nose. Everybody's fat, from Falstaff's to Zero Mostel's, is funny. And when the deformity is functional rather than organic it continues to be funny. Stuttering and lisping are two of the swiftest, most indestructible sources of laughter in the entire low-comedy canon; occasionally we think ourselves above such devices, and reformers are apt to scorn them as antisocial and cruel; the fact remains that there is scarcely a high-school comedy produced in the land that does not lean on them, while the sophisticated professional theater simply translates lisping into effeminacy and continues to go its merry, utterly standardized way.

WALTER KERR, *Tragedy and Comedy*

A paragraph can move from one phase of an idea to another as long as both phases are clearly linked and the relation between the two is part of the central theme. The third paragraph in the passage by Frederick Lewis Allen (page 198) illustrates this structure. The following paragraph presents a contrast which begins with the third sentence; the two parts are necessary in discussing the relationship between art and feeling.

The work of art is in some sense a liberation of the personality; normally our feelings are inhibited and repressed. We contemplate a work of art, and immediately there is a release; and not only a release—sympathy is a release of feelings—but also a heightening, a tautening, a sublimation. Here is the essential difference between art and sentimentality: sentimentality is a release, but also a loosening, a relaxing of the emotions; art is a release, but also a bracing. Art is the economy of feeling; it is emotion cultivating good form.

HERBERT READ, *The Meaning of Art*

Exercise 1

Three topic sentences are given for each of the paragraphs below. One is the actual topic sentence written by the author. The other two are less exact. Read each paragraph carefully, determine the central unity of thought, and pick out the best topic sentence.

A

1. Few people read enough poetry to define it accurately.
2. Few poets have defined poetry accurately.
3. Few people have ever been brave enough to define poetry.

Not many among those few have felt happy with their definitions. Yet most of us have experienced poetry, and many of us believe that we can recognize it when we see it, just as we can recognize life when we see it, although we cannot satisfactorily define it. Like life, poetry exists in so many forms and on so many levels that it triumphantly defies description. Keats has written of poetry as the realms of gold, and has noted its many goodly states and kingdoms, its many islands held in fealty to Apollo. The metaphor is a good one, though it hardly goes far enough. There are more poems than there are islands in the Caribbean, or the Mediterranean; and they vary more in shape, size, color, contour, and human habitability.

DONALD A. STAUFFER, The Nature of Poetry

B

1. The problem of the origin of corn cannot be easily solved, for the wild forms of corn so far discovered do not match modern domesticated species.
2. The problem of the origin of corn has been ignored by historians and scientists alike.
3. The problem of the origin of corn has intrigued botanists and other students of plants for more than four centuries.

The plant was unknown in any part of the Old World before 1492, while in the New World it was the basic food plant of all pre-Columbian advanced cultures and civilizations, including the Inca of South America and the Maya and Aztec of Middle America. Although these facts point strongly to its American origin, some writers have continued to argue eloquently for an Old World origin. A living wild form of corn has never been discovered, despite the extensive searches for it which have been carried on in various parts of the hemisphere. The absence of a wild form has been conducive to speculation — sometimes reaching the point of acrimonious debate — about its probable nature. There has, however, been general agreement that modern corn is unique among the major cereals in its grain-bearing inflorescence (the ear), which is completely enclosed in modified leaf sheaths (the husks), the plant being thus rendered incapable of dispersing its seeds. How, then, did wild corn, which to survive in nature must have had a means of dispersal, differ from modern cultivated corn? Where did it grow? How did it evolve under domestication? These are some of the questions that comprise the corn problem.

P. C. MANGELSDORF, R. S. MACNEISH, W. C. GALINAT,
"Domestication of Corn"

C

1. These little, private, church-based colleges are an important part of American smalltown life.
2. These little, private, church-based colleges have given up all their traditions.
3. These little, private, church-based colleges are an unattractive part of American smalltown life.

They were founded by all the various religious sects during the nineteenth century, and having one established in your own growing town was a matter for civic pride, like getting piped water. They used to teach theology. Now they offer a four-year Liberal Arts course and worry about the prestige of their football team like anyone else. (A successful team attracts new students and they all need the fees, urgently.) For the same reason, they have to defer to the students' progressive views to a certain extent. Religious services are no longer compulsory and students in need of an abortion will think first of consulting the chaplain. But none of these colleges has completely shaken off the duty to teach character-training as well as subject matter.

RUTH ADAM, "Smalltown America"

D

1. Schools do not have to be unpleasant places.
2. Schools can be humane and still educate well.
3. Schools of the future will use fewer teachers.

They can be genuinely concerned with gaiety and joy and individual growth and fulfillment without sacrificing concern for intellectual discipline and development. They can be simultaneously child-centered and subject- or knowledge-centered. They can stress aesthetic and moral education without weakening the three R's. They can do all these things if — but only if — their structure, content, and objectives are transformed.

CHARLES E. SILBERMAN, "Murder in the Schoolroom"

E

1. Formal schools do not educate good students as well as informal schools.
2. Schools must be innovative in many ways.
3. There is a conviction that learning is likely to be more effective if it grows out of what interests the learner, rather than what interests the teacher.

This is a truism to any adult: we *know* how rapidly we can learn something that really interests us, and how long it takes to master something which bores us, or for which we have a positive distaste. Formal schools, whether in England or the United States, tend to ignore the truism; informal schools do not. Hence they generally abandon the traditional rigid timetable which divides the day into a succession of short periods. In its place there are longer periods, during which, at the teacher's discretion and under his supervision, students may be engaged individually or in small groups in a wide variety of activities.

CHARLES E. SILBERMAN, "Murder in the Schoolroom"

F

1. By the end of the 1960's, scientists and laymen were hopeful that biology would enable man to achieve wonderful things.
2. By the end of the 1960's, scientists and laymen alike were conscious of living in a biological revolution.
3. By the end of the 1960's, scientists and laymen alike lived in great fear of the consequences of a biological revolution.

No one could confidently say that the good consequences for human happiness would outweigh the bad,
and many people feared the opposite. Biology as an
escape from the ethical dilemmas of nuclear physics
turned out to be another dream of innocence gone
aglimmering. The undercurrents of anxiety liberated
by this development have now surfaced in the extraor-
dinary press conference held by the team of research-
ers in the Harvard Medical School, led by Jonathan
Beckwith, to warn the world against the possible abuse
of their own triumph in isolating the first gene.

DONALD FLEMING, "Big Science Under Fire"

G

1. If something is not done soon, our civilization will lose
   all its traditions.
2. No civilization can live without ideals, or to put it another way, without a firm faith in moral ideas.
3. Religion may be a sham to some and a crutch to others,
   but without a firm faith in God our everyday lives can
   be but empty—that has always been the case and certainly always will be.

Our ideals and moral ideas have in the past been root-
ed in religion. But the religious basis of our ideals has
been undermined, and the superstructure of ideals is
plainly tottering. None of the commonly suggested
remedies on examination seems likely to succeed. It
would therefore look as if the early death of our civilization were inevitable.

W. T. STACE, "Man Against Darkness"

H

1. The intention to make money is generally all too obvious.
2. They do not make movies like they used to.
3. More people ought to go to the movies.

One of the excruciating comedies of our time is attending the new classes in cinema at the high schools where the students may quite shrewdly and accurately interpret the plot developments in a mediocre movie in terms of manipulation for a desired response while the teacher tries to explain everything in terms of the creative artist working out his theme — as if the conditions under which a movie is made and the market for which it is designed were irrelevant, as if the latest product from Warners or Universal should be analyzed like a lyric poem.

PAULINE KAEL, "Trash, Art, and the Movies"

I

1. Man should stop worrying about pollution and go on about his business.
2. Man is not on his way to extinction.
3. Despite great changes, man always makes the best of his environment.

He can adapt to almost anything. I am sure that we can adapt to the dirt, pollution and the noise of New York City or Chicago. That is the real tragedy — we can adapt to it. As we become adapted we accept worse and worse conditions without realizing that a child born and raised in this environment has no chance of developing his total physical and mental potential. It is essential that we commit ourselves to such problems as a society and as a nation, not because we are threatened with extinction, but because, if we do not understand what the environment is doing to us, something perhaps worse than extinction will take place — a progressive degradation of the quality of human life.

RENE DUBOS, "We Can't Buy Our Way Out"

J

1. *Playboy* magazine is among the best literature of our age.
2. In *Playboy* magazine life is vastly misrepresented.
3. Both the image of man and the means for its attainment exhibit a remarkable consistency in *Playboy*.

The skilled consumer is cool and unruffled. He savors sports cars, liquor, high fidelity, and book-club selections with a casual, unhurried aplomb. Though he must certainly *have* and *use* the latest consumption item, he must not permit himself to get too attached to it. The style will change and he must always be ready to adjust. His persistent anxiety that he may mix a drink incorrectly, enjoy a jazz group that is passé, or wear last year's necktie style is comforted by an authoritative tone in *Playboy* beside which papal encyclicals sound irresolute.

HARVEY COX, "The Playboy and Miss America"

K

1. Patriotism can be defined as a dogmatic or even religious faith in one's own country.
2. Modern events usually have little influence on the way a country thinks because times and fads change so rapidly.
3. One way in which a nation defines itself is by its attitudes to its own past.

Most countries glorify past events and aspirations and in the process create certain inflated standards or artificial norms which they use to evaluate and revise the present. Such measures or gauges we usually call tradition, custom, convention, or myth. When these standards or attitudes are applied to contemporary events, they frequently confer a patriotic or nationalistic tone. Generally, the shakier a regime, or the more dishonest its position, the more forcefully it recalls its past, whether as glory or as shame.

FREDERICK R. KARL, "The Uselessness of the Past"

45c Use enough details to explain or support your ideas and to keep your reader interested.

Do not write paragraphs which sketch only the outlines of a topic. The following paragraph does not go beyond generalities:

Wit is individual and sometimes malicious, whereas humor belongs to a group and is usually peaceful. Wit is fashionable, but humor is homely. Usually there is a victim of wit, but not of humor. Also, humor provokes laughter but wit is the prod-uct of study. This is a sad workaday world, and the humorous are better company than the witty.

In the following, Charles S. Brooks develops the same idea fully and effectively by the use of concrete, vivid descriptive details.

Wit is a lean creature with sharp inquiring nose, whereas humor has a kindly eye and comfortable girth. Wit, if it be necessary, uses malice to score a point—like a cat it is quick to jump—but humor keeps the peace in an easy chair. Wit has a better voice in a solo, but humor comes into the chorus best. Wit is as sharp as a stroke of lightning, whereas humor is diffuse like sunlight. Wit keeps the season's fashions and is precise in the phrases and judgments of the day, but humor is concerned with homely eternal things. Wit wears silk, but humor in homespun endures the wind. Wit sets a snare, whereas humor goes off whistling without a victim in its mind. Wit is sharper company at table, but humor serves better in mischance and in the rain. When it tumbles, wit is sour, but humor goes uncomplaining without its dinner. Humor laughs at another's jest and holds its sides, while wit sits wrapped in study for a lively answer. But it is a workaday world in which we live, where we get mud upon our boots and come weary to the twilight—it is a world that grieves and suffers from many wounds in these years of war: and therefore as I think of my acquaintance, it is those who are humorous in its best and truest meaning rather than those who are witty who give the more profitable companionship.

CHARLES S. BROOKS, "On the Difference Between Wit and Humor"

Write about things you know, and remember the small telling details which can make even abstractions like wit and humor seem to have flesh and blood.

45d Develop a paragraph by the method most appropriate for the central topic.

Paragraphs may develop their topics in many ways. They may define, classify, move from cause to effect or effect to cause, from a generalization to the facts it interprets, from a body of facts to a generalization about them. Usually the material on a subject so clearly dictates its pattern that the writer does not even have to decide that he will write a paragraph of a certain kind—definition, for example. He simply defines without deciding to do so, because defining is what his material demands. He thinks about his subject and material, and the method takes care of itself. There are, however, a few points to keep in mind.

Climactic Order Any list can be made more interesting if you begin with the least important item and end with the most important.

Comparison and Contrast Two basic methods can be used in developing a paragraph by comparison and contrast: writing everything about one point and then everything about the other (XXXX YYYY); or writing about alternating points throughout the paragraph (XY XY XY XY). Either method can be effective, but in long and complex comparisons and contrasts the alternating method is generally better. If an entire theme is a comparison and contrast, avoid devoting half of the theme to one side of the comparison and the other half to the other.

Definition Good expository definition tries to explain an abstraction clearly and accurately. The problem is to make the term sufficiently concrete in examples which do not excessively restrict the meaning. Intellectual definitions, of course, may be much more elaborate than the definitions given in dictionaries.

45e Use transitions to show relationships between sentences within paragraphs and between one paragraph and another.

Transitional devices help a reader see how and why you progress from one point to another and how your ideas are related.

Connective Words and Expressions

but	indeed	likewise
and	in fact	consequently
however	meanwhile	first
moreover	afterward	next
furthermore	then	in brief
on the other hand	so	to summarize
nevertheless	still	to conclude
for example	after all	similarly

Demonstratives (References must be clear.)
> this   that   these   those

Other Pronouns
> many   each   some   others   such   either

Repeated Key Words, Phrases, and Synonyms

Repetitions and synonyms are good signposts to guide the reader from sentence to sentence and paragraph to paragraph.

Transitional words in topic sentences can contribute materially to clarity, coherence, and the movement of the discussion. Some writers meticulously guide readers with a connector at the beginning of almost every paragraph. H. J. Muller, for example, begins a sequence of paragraphs about science as follows:

> In this summary, science . . .
> Yet science does . . .
> Similarly the basic interests of science . . .
> In other words, they are not . . .
> This demonstration that even the scientist . . .
> This idea will concern us . . .
> In other words, facts and figures . . .

Exercise 2

Refer to Exercise 1 on pages 200–208. For each paragraph describe the method of development, use of details, and use of transitional devices.

45f Avoid choppy paragraphs and excessively long paragraphs.

Paragraphs vary in length from a single word to a page or more. Short paragraphs allow a reader to grasp facts quickly and easily. But in complex material, they can chop up related ideas or dismiss ideas before they are properly developed.

A series of short, choppy paragraphs may suggest underdeveloped ideas expressed in two or three sentences apiece. If closely related in thought, such paragraphs can often be combined into longer ones, each with a good topic sentence. If not closely related, each may be expanded to make a true paragraph, or some may be omitted.

Short paragraphs are sometimes standard and effective in news items, fiction, dialogue, and descriptions of dramatic action. The length of a paragraph is usually decided by the importance and complexity of its central idea, the richness of detail that develops it, and even the number of words allowed in an assignment. Paragraphs in a theme of 300 words will generally be shorter and more uniform in length than those in a theme of 700 words, and certainly shorter than those in a paper of 1500 to 2000 words. Thought should never be divided into paragraphs simply at mechanical intervals.

The following selection is chopped up excessively, and its divisions are not logical.

But perhaps we should beware of taking evidence of this sort too tragically, or of deducing from detective stories nothing but a pessimistic moral. The condemnation of detective stories as drugs or cheap escapism may be pedantic.

For, if they are a symptom, they can also be a cure. If we credit the Freudian view that socially dangerous impulses can be got rid of by removing them to the level of fantasy, then detective stories could be described as a harmless safety valve, a wholesome therapy serving a desirable social purpose.

And yet one may wonder if this commonly accepted view is entirely correct, if fantasy and real life are actually so unrelated.

To some extent we may build our real life around our fantasy and, if this is so, sensation literature may not so much rid us of dangerous drives as reinforce and reshape them.

In any case, if detective stories are not so sinister as they at first appear from analysis, neither are they as frivolous as some critics have judged them.

The drives they cater to are compelling and basic, and relate ultimately to the struggle for self-preservation. It is the universal nature of their theme which explains the size and variety of their reading audience. The intellectual, who scorns the cheap fantasies of the popular magazines, is not likely to be able to forgo the fantasies which give him hope for his survival in an alien world.

Detective stories deal, in their own way and on their own level, with the most essential and urgent problems in the human condition.

ADAPTED FROM WILLIAM O. AYDELOTTE, "The Detective Story
as a Historical Source"

Actually the above passage was written as two paragraphs, the second beginning with the sentence "In any case, if detective. . . ." Notice that this sentence makes an excellent transition: the first part looks back to the previous paragraph, and the rest introduces the new thought. When the passage is divided properly into two paragraphs, continuity is improved and the logic of the thought becomes clearer.

But perhaps we should beware of taking evidence of this sort too tragically, or of deducing from detective stories nothing but a pessimistic moral. The condemnation of detective stories as drugs or cheap escapism may be pedantic. For, if they are a symptom, they can also be a cure. If we credit the Freudian view that socially dangerous impulses can be got rid of by removing them to the level of fantasy, then detective stories could be described as a harmless safety valve, a wholesome therapy serving a desirable social purpose. And yet one may wonder if this commonly accepted view is entirely correct, if fantasy and real life are actually so unrelated. To some extent we may build our real life around our fantasy and, if this is so, sensation literature may not so much rid us of dangerous drives as reinforce and reshape them.

In any case, if detective stories are not so sinister as they at first appear from analysis, neither are they as frivolous as some critics have judged them. The drives they cater to are compelling and basic, and relate ultimately to the struggle for self-preservation. It is the universal nature of their theme which explains the size and variety of their reading audience. The intellectual, who scorns the cheap fantasies of the popular magazines, is not likely to be able to forgo the fantasies which give him hope for his survival in an alien world. Detective stories deal, in their own way and on their own level, with the most essential and urgent problems in the human condition.

Very long paragraphs make it hard for a reader to digest meaning easily. To reduce excessive length it may be necessary to reduce the scope of the controlling idea—to limit purpose. But sometimes a paragraph can be trimmed simply by discarding material. You may not need ten examples to prove or illustrate a point. Four or five may do it just as well.

Exercise 3

The following sentences have been changed from their original sequence within the paragraph. By the use of numbers written at the left of the sentences, indicate their original order as you conceive it. Be ready to defend your decisions. The paragraphs themselves are presented in their original sequence.[1]

Paragraph One

As representatives of remote and militant Indian tribes, they were there as objects of an elaborate scheme designed to influence them to accept peaceably American expansion into their country.

---

[1] These passages, scrambled for educational purposes, have been adapted from "Invitation to Washington—A Bid for Peace," by Herman J. Viola, *The American West*, January, 1972; reprinted here by permission of the publisher.

Each year, as generations of curious Americans have done before them, thousands of visitors file through the rooms and hallways of the White House.

Ironically, one hundred and fifty years ago these Indians were also White House visitors, gaping in wonderment and fascination at all they saw.

They were no ordinary tourists.

Few leave without a renewed feeling for the dignity of America's cultural heritage—a feeling enhanced by five striking Indian portraits that hang in the ground-floor library.

Paragraph Two

Inviting Indian leaders to visit America's most important cities, especially Washington, D.C., was a major component of this policy.

The Indians whose portraits now hang in the White House library were no exceptions when, in the fall of 1821, they were brought to Washington by their agent Benjamin O'Fallon.

After inspecting forts, arsenals, and battleships, being showered with presents, and meeting their Great Father the president, few of the impressionable natives returned to their people without profound respect for the wealth and strength of the United States.

Too weak to risk war with the powerful tribes arrayed along its western borders, the federal government until well into the nineteenth century stressed diplomacy rather than force in its Indian policy.

Paragraph Three

As Calhoun explained in the letter appointing O'Fallon agent, "The important military movements which are contemplated on the Missouri will be greatly facilitated or impeded by the friendship or hostilities of the Indians. Their disposition will be principally influenced by the conduct of the agent, and you will accordingly spare no pains to acquire their friendship and confidence."

Two years earlier, O'Fallon had been given the task of preparing the Indians of the Upper Missouri region for the arrival of the Americans. Fearful of England's intentions in the Northwest following the War of 1812, Secretary of War John C. Calhoun had conceived a master plan intended to overawe the tribes and cut off their intercourse with British traders operating from Canada.

Calhoun assured O'Fallon that "these important objects" could be accomplished by a proper combination of kindness, firmness, and "a judicious distribution of presents."

A military post was to be established on the Missouri River at its confluence with the Yellowstone, and another at the mouth of the Minnesota on the Mississippi, thereby securing the vast area of the two river valleys for American interests.

The devastating depression of 1819 and a cost-conscious Congress shattered Calhoun's plans for western expansion, leaving Fort Atkinson and the Upper Missouri Indian Agency, established at Council Bluffs, the exposed vanguards of the United States.

Exercise 4

One sentence has been added to each of the following paragraphs in such a way as to affect paragraph unity. Identify each of the foreign sentences.

Fermentation is that particular bio-chemical wonder in which tiny living creatures called yeasts gobble up sugar and starch and turn them into alcohol and carbon dioxide. In baking, the carbon dioxide, trapped in the sticky, elastic dough made with wheat or rye flour, collects in little pockets which then swell and form air holes in the bread, thus leavening it. Only wheat or rye flour contains the necessary gluten to make the dough sticky and elastic enough to trap the carbon dioxide. The baking fixes the air holes permanently in the bread, cooks off the alcohol, and kills the yeast cells, thus preventing further fermentation. When I was a girl, I remember well the pleasures of eating just-baked bread.

The yeast cells first used by man are called wild yeasts, and like people, they have been evolving through the years. Scientists speak of "new races" and "mutations" of them. The particular wild yeast cells used by the ancients to make bread were probably the same as those they used to ferment honey, grape juice, and grain mash to make mead, wine, and beer. Some anthropologists even believe that making alcohol from fermented grain predates agriculture—that man, in fact, took to the hoe in order to take to his cups. Beer halls all over the country are full each evening, and there is some doubt about the advantages of legalized alcohol. Whether or not that is so, man was almost certainly a brewer before he was a baker.

Since wild yeast cells are always present in nature, carried by insects or on specks of dust, it is possible to start a *levain* by mixing together flour and water and simply setting the mixture outdoors, uncovered, on a warm humid day. This method can be improved upon by the addition to the mixture of some crushed ripe grapes. California currently is one of the great grape producers of the country. With irrepressible conviviality, wild yeast cells tend to congregate on the skins of ripe grapes. There they wait impatiently for some bare foot or mechanical winepress to break the grape skin and let them in. With or without smashed grapes, however, the flour and water mixture will attract its own yeasts, ferment, and foam. It must then be built up with successive feedings of flour and water and allowed to ferment and foam several more times until it has developed enough yeast cells to give rise to a batch of bread.

BETTY SUYKER, "A la Recherche du Pain Perdu"

Exercise 5

A

The author divided the following passage into three paragraphs. Indicate the places where you believe he made the divisions and underline the topic sentences.

Each language spoken by man (there are over 2,800) is honeycombed with uniqueness. Human languages are as different as peas in a pod (if you examined them under a microscope). What human tongues have in common is only purpose: the use of words to try to describe, understand,

and communicate the measureless sensations of existence, the swarm of impressions on the self, the marvelous symbolic productions of the human mind, the infinite fantasies of the imagination, the divine and the wretched parameters of the human condition. A language is a *Weltanschauung*. Even languages very close in origin, history, and structure develop surprising differences. The English "conscience" is not the same as the French *conscience* (which means consciousness or conscientiousness). German had no word for "bully" until the twentieth century (a mordant comment on Teutonic values) and can only render the Englishman's idea of "fair play" as *"fair" Spielen*. If this be true of tongues so close to each other in birth, so laden with cognates, so cross-fertilized by usage and literature, how much more does it intrude when one tries to translate Yiddish or Hebrew into any of them? Translation is not simply a matter of dexterity in transferring synonyms. Translation does not contend with words, but with meanings. To translate is to decode: to transpose one mode of thinking, feeling, fearing, appraising into the word-patterns of another. No language can be separated from its historical skeleton, its psychological skin, or its sociological garments. Languages are acculturated verbalizations of experience and thought.

LEO ROSTEN, "The Torments of Translation: Dismantling the Tower of Babel"

B

The author divided the following passage into five paragraphs. Indicate the places where you believe she made the divisions.

Almost two-thirds of American women live in cities. In relation to the total population, one-tenth of all white people are poor, but about one-third of all blacks are poor. Out of every ten poor persons, four are children. More than one family in ten is headed by a woman; there are 5.6 million such families in the United States, of which 43 per cent are headed by widows and 46 per cent by divorced or separated women. About two million of these families are below the poverty level. While the number of poor families headed by men dropped by half between 1959 and 1969, the number of poor families headed by women has remained virtually unchanged. The hardest hit family is the one headed by a black woman who works; 45 per cent of these families live in poverty compared to 16 per cent headed by a male black worker. Three-fifths of the 3.4 million families headed by a woman with children under 18 need some financial assistance. Most women hold a high school diploma. Of the women in the age group 20 to 24, 80 per cent were high school graduates in 1970, as were men in the same age group. But relatively few women have earned a college degree. In 1970 the per cent of all women over 21 who had been through four or more years of college was 9 per cent compared to 14 per cent for men. The widest gap, however, between men and women's education appears at the professional level. Only 9 per cent of all scientists are women, 7 per cent of all physicians, 3 per cent of lawyers and just 1 per cent of engineers and federal judges. The per cent of women on college faculties has declined from 28 per cent in 1922 to 22 per cent in 1940. In the 92nd Congress there was one female Senator. In the House twelve women held seats out of a possible 435; this is only two more than served in the 91st Congress and only one is a black woman. Early in 1969 eleven women were occupying federal judgeships by Presidential appointment. The number of women in state legislatures declined from 370 in 1965 to 318 in 1967, and now stands at about 300. Sixty-two per cent of American women are married. Most women marry young, on an average just before their 21st birthday. There is not only a rush to be a June bride but to be married by 21; after that a woman is an old maid capable only of feeling sorry for herself that she has failed somehow in the "sweepstakes of life." Approximately 27 per cent of American women marry younger than 21, between 14 and 19 years of age. It is not surprising then that the rate for disrupted marriages, those marriages ending in divorce or separation, is increasing and shows no immediate sign of declining. In 1970, 10 per cent of all married women were so affected. For young women between 20 and 24, the number of disrupted marriages has increased about 25 per cent since 1960.

JACQUELINE ST. JOHN, "Women's Legislative Issues
Today and Tomorrow"

46 Writing Good Themes

There are stages in the process of composition which overlap but can be separated for discussion. These include choosing and limiting a subject; determining your purpose and planning the development of your paper, often through an outline; writing the first draft; revising and preparing the final draft. Except for impromptu class assignments, a good paper is seldom written at a single sitting. Depending on the time at your disposal, planning and gathering material can extend over days or even weeks.

46a Choose a subject that interests you.

To find significant and interesting subjects, draw on your experience, memory, imagination, knowledge, interests, and study.

Good subjects can come to mind at unexpected moments. You may think of one while your thoughts are wandering in class or while you are taking your clothes to the laundry. Never let a possible subject escape you. Reserve a page or two in your notebook for all the topics and titles which occur to you. Even the less promising possibilities may evolve into good subjects. When a theme must be written, it is better to have an excess of ideas than a blank sheet of paper staring at you from your desk. You can avoid false starts and lost time by examining your list of possibilities and settling on one good topic at the outset. (For suggestions about subjects for themes, see pp. 242–245.)

46b Limit the subject appropriately.

Tailor your topic to the length of the assignment. Do not skim the surface of a broad subject, but select a limited part of it and develop that part fully through discussion, analysis, illustration, and detail.

A 250-word paper calls for a more limited treatment than a 500-word or a 1000-word paper; it may demand a different subject altogether. Generalized treatments of large subjects can be successful if they are handled with intelligence, breadth of perspective, and insight; many good editorials are written on just such topics. But the best themes usually treat topics limited enough to allow room for plenty of explanation and detail.

Suppose a student starts with the idea of writing a 500-word theme on "some physical activity." On the opposite page, the evolution of his subject is shown in the column at the left; the student's thoughts about each subject are suggested at the right.

The mind plays curious tricks. Through association of ideas—physical activity, athletics, work, recreation involving hard work—this student arrived at a suitably limited subject, and it is a good subject because it evidently derives from an experience significant to him. Letting the mind range in this way helps to limit a subject by relating it to live interests of your own.

Even after the topic is thus limited, you cannot *know* that it is the right size until you have (1) considered its subdivisions and (2) sometimes actually written the theme. A subject which at first seems limited may open up into greater complexity and promise to yield a paper

SUBJECT	THOUGHTS ABOUT SUBJECT
Some physical activity	*Too broad . . .*
Athletics	*Too broad . . . not much interested . . . no inspiration . . .*
Work	*Again too broad . . . but might have something here . . . toss the subject around a little . . .*
The unpleasantness of some kind of hard labor	*Sounds unpleasant . . . unattractive topic equals unattractive theme? . . .*
Hard labor can be enjoyable	*But do I really believe this? Could I convince a reader? . . .*
Labor connected with a hobby	*We don't mind hard work, even get fun out of it, if it ties up with something we enjoy . . .*
Making a raft	*But just making it isn't much fun . . .*
Using a raft	*Getting close . . .*
Downriver on a raft	*Subject at last!*

far beyond the assigned length. If so you must turn to another subject—perhaps a still more limited aspect of the first.

Or if the paper is already written you may reduce the length of it, usually by cutting out whole sections. But a theme shortened in this way is often confused, jerky, or badly proportioned because of omissions and condensations. A fresh start with a new topic may cost a high price in lost time. It is much better to write a theme of the proper length in the first place.

46c **Formulate your controlling purpose or thesis statement.**

The central idea of a paper can usually be expressed in a single sentence. Sometimes this statement can be phrased early in the planning process, sometimes not until you are near the actual writing. In any event, it should be expressed or clearly implied early in the written paper, often in the opening paragraph.

A good **thesis statement** is specific and concise. It defines the scope of the paper and the writer's approach. It brings the subject into focus and promises the reader a single, definite idea to control the rest of the paper.

VAGUE It is the purpose of this paper to discuss the nature of jokes.

VAGUE Good jokes have qualities in common.

MORE PURPOSEFUL Nearly all good jokes contain an element of surprise or perhaps even a momentary shock.

46d **Select a tone (or mood) appropriate to the topic.**

At some point in the planning, as you gather material and clarify purpose, you will be able to decide what you want the tone of your paper to be. **Tone** is the quality which reveals the writer's attitude toward his subject matter. Writing may be serious or humorous, ironical or straightforward, zealous or casual, brisk or nostalgic. The tone need not be held unvaryingly in one key—it may, for example, move reasonably from the serious to a touch of humor—but it should not run from one extreme to another in the same piece of writing. An inconsistent tone confuses a reader about the writer's intention.

A writer should avoid flippancy or sarcasm which reveals contempt for his subject (see §44i) or for his reader.

46e Organize and develop your paper carefully.

Concurrently with choosing and limiting a subject, formulating a thesis, and establishing tone, you will be gathering material and putting it in order. At an early stage, it may look like this:

Work	Hobbies
Play	Relaxation
Not enough time	Idleness
Too much time	Retirement
More leisure now than ever before	Faster transportation
	Time-saving
What to do with it	"Time on My Hands"
Shorter working hours	Ordering one's life
Wasting time	Using common sense
Planned leisure	Some still without leisure
Frustration and leisure	Creativity
Too much TV	Value of work
Improving the mind	Good and bad entertainment

These topics may be the basic materials for a theme, but they hardly resemble the final product. The steps between this listing of topics and the writing process are never the same for any two papers. One good way to proceed is to start writing notes about particular topics even before trying to give them order. Full notes can often be put together into a paper with only arrangement, revision, and a few additions.

A more conventional way is to prepare a formal outline before the paper is really begun. This process rearranges topics, puts them in coherent groups, decides which comes first, determines the major topics and the subheadings. Few people can really proceed in orderly fashion from topics to outline to the paper itself. Most papers result from some kind of combination of these methods.

Getting from the notes and the outline to the introduction is probably the single most crucial step. Sometimes it takes as long to write the first paragraph as to write all the rest of the paper. It is not unusual to have to throw away the first three or four starts. When a writer finally arrives at the first good statement of his introduction and his thesis sentence, he then sees the larger meaning of his work. The introduction really defines the topic, which is merely named in the title; and thereafter every paragraph must **make its own contribution** and at the same time look back to the thesis sentence and **state its connection to the over-all topic.**

46f Develop a topic outline as you organize your thinking. Your instructor may require that you write a topic or a sentence outline for a paper. (See §46g for the sentence outline.)

The **topic outline** follows certain conventions. Avoid general headings such as "Introduction," "Body," "Conclusion." These do not specify any real content.

1. Number the main topics with Roman numerals, the first subheadings with capital letters, the next with Arabic numerals. If further subheadings are necessary—though they seldom are for short papers—use a, b, c, and (1), (2), (3).

```
I. ............................................
    A. .......................................
        1. ...................................
            a. ...............................
                (1) ..........................
                (2) ..........................
            b. ...............................
        2. ...................................
    B. .......................................
II. ............................................
```

2. Use parallel grammatical structures.

3. Use topics, not sentences. Do not place periods after the topics. Punctuate as above.

4. Check to see that your outline covers the subject completely.

5. Use specific topics and subheadings arranged in a logical, meaningful order. Each indented level of the outline represents a division of the preceding level and has smaller scope.

Avoid single subheadings.

NOT   I. Man's long search for leisure
           A. The past
       II. Advantages of leisure

Roman numeral I calls for II; subheading A calls for B, and so forth.

The following is an example of a topic outline with a title, a thesis statement, and a series of orderly and carefully developed topics. A short paper may require a less elaborate outline than this.

THE AGE OF LEISURE

Thesis Statement: Man, who has long searched for leisure time, has found it, but with it have come serious problems that must be solved.

I. Man's long search for leisure
    A. The past
        1. Leisure the privilege of only the upper class
        2. Overwork and the stifling of the human spirit
        3. Persistence of the dream: escape from toil
    B. Modern times—leisure for the masses
        1. Exceptions—those still without leisure
        2. Changes for the worker
            a. Shorter work week
            b. Longer vacations
            c. Earlier retirement
        3. Time-saving devices in the home
        4. Jet-age transportation
II. Advantages of leisure
    A. To the individual
        1. The full life
            a. Improvement of the mind
            b. Travel
            c. Creativity
        2. Relaxation and health
    B. To society
        1. Volunteer services
        2. Opportunities for closer family and social ties
III. Dangers of excessive leisure
    A. Wasted leisure
        1. Ignorance of available opportunities for constructive leisure
        2. Unrewarding entertainment
            a. The "movie rut"
            b. The "TV trance"

B. Leisure and human nature
1. Leisure or laziness?
2. Loss of direction through excessive leisure
3. Free time and frustration
   a. Man's innate desire for orderly life
   b. Prisoners who are afraid to leave prison
C. Leisure and the destruction of traditional values
1. Dignity of honest toil
2. Idleness and evil
IV. Survival in the age of leisure
A. Recognizing the problems
B. Forming the proper attitudes
1. Compatibility of work and leisure
2. Maturity and common sense
C. Improving the opportunity for leisure
1. Planned but not unnatural leisure
2. Education and leisure
3. Better entertainment

46g Develop a sentence outline as you organize your thinking.

The **sentence outline** follows the same conventions as the topic outline except that the entries are all expressed in complete sentences. Place periods after sentences in a sentence outline.

THE AGE OF LEISURE

Thesis Statement: Man, who has long searched for leisure time, has found it, but with it have come serious problems that must be solved.

I. Man has searched for leisure time as long as he has existed.
- A. In the past, leisure was rare.
  - 1. Leisure was the privilege of only the upper class.
  - 2. For the common man, overwork has frequently stifled the human spirit.
  - 3. Nevertheless, man's dream has stubbornly persisted through the centuries: to escape from toil.
- B. Today the common man has more leisure time than he ever had before.
  - 1. Some exceptions, however, remain: those who are still deprived of leisure time.
  - 2. For most workers many changes have provided much free time.
    - a. The work week is shorter.
    - b. Vacations are generally longer.
    - c. Workers are able to retire earlier.
  - 3. In the home new devices are saving the housewife time which can be spent in leisure.
  - 4. Much time is also saved through modern means of transportation.

II. Several advantages of leisure are apparent.
    A. The individual gains much from leisure.
        1. Leisure enables one to live a full and rich life.
            a. Through leisure one has the opportunity to improve his mind.
            b. Using leisure time to travel broadens one's perspective.
            c. Leisure offers the chance for exercising creative talents.
        2. Leisure can lead to greater relaxation and health.
    B. Many advantages accrue to society through the increase in leisure.
        1. People have more time to give to various volunteer services.
        2. There are greater opportunities for closer family and social ties.
III. Excessive leisure carries with it a great number of serious dangers.
    A. Since leisure time is now plentiful, many people waste it.
        1. Much wasted leisure is caused by an ignorance of the available opportunities.
        2. Others waste their leisure on unrewarding forms of entertainment.
            a. Thousands of people are content to spend their time in a "movie rut," watching shallow motion pictures without content or value.
            b. Others sit at home hour after hour in front of the television set, as if in a trance.
    B. Other dangers are present because of certain aspects of human nature.
        1. Leisure sometimes leads to laziness.
        2. Unless our goals are kept constantly before us, excessive leisure can cause loss of direction.

3. Because of man's psychological make-up, too much free time frequently brings on frustration.

    a. Man seems to have an innate desire for a well-organized, orderly life.

    b. An example of how free time can bring frustration can be seen in the case of some prisoners who fear to leave prison because they cannot organize their time.

C. Leisure also presents a danger to many traditional values.

  1. The old belief that there is dignity in honest toil becomes endangered.

  2. Many believe that too much leisure produces idleness, upon which evil thrives.

IV. If man is to survive in the modern age of leisure, he must face and solve the problems.

A. First of all, the problems presented by great leisure must be recognized.

B. Man must form the proper attitudes.

  1. To prevent fragmentation in his life, he must learn to blend work and leisure.

  2. He must rely on maturity and common sense to control his leisure.

C. Man must work to improve the opportunities for leisure.

  1. Leisure time should be carefully planned but never unnatural.

  2. Education must keep pace with increased leisure.

  3. The public should demand better entertainment worthy of its leisure.

46h Use varied details for interest, illustration, explanation, or proof. (See also § 45c.)

An abstract truth may be evident in a concrete example or action. Sometimes it is enough to state the concrete fact, omit the general truth, and let the reader reach the abstract conclusion for himself. Ultimately, meaningful generalizations rest on details.

The sentence on the left below is thin, vague, general, lacking in detail. The passage on the right shows how the same point may be developed with specific detail.

Early immigrants from Europe to America came in ships that seemed sturdy in the harbor but fragile on the sea.

The New World began at the water's edge in Europe.

Tiny vessels, sixty to two hundred tons in the main, bore the voyagers westward. Riding at anchor in the sheltered bays of the homeland, the ships seemed substantial enough. Their sturdy timber and looming masts, their cabins that rose like a castle several stories high in the stern, were impressive in comparison with the harbor craft that flitted about them. At sea, it would be another matter. All became precarious as the isolated specks, buffeted by the elements, beat their way into the unknown immensity before them; and the men below huddled fearfully in the cramped space that set their condition of life. (Oscar Handlin, *The Americans*)

Exercise

*Read the following selections. The first is a student theme;
the second, the introductory part of an article from* The
New York Times Magazine. *Be prepared to outline each
and to discuss its interest, the way its author has limited
his subject, its organization, and use of details.*

THE BLUFFTON HOUSE

To me, Bluffton Farm is synonymous with vacation
time, and its outstanding feature is the forty-year-old
house. It sits back in a grove of pines and palmettos, looking like an ugly duckling between the modern, two-story
brick houses of my aunt and uncle. It is built of heart-of-
pine lumber, which has no paint—and never has had. A
once-red roof covers the long structure.

A rusted screen porch, which runs the full length of the
house, is notable by itself. It is furnished with Army surplus cots covered with khaki cloth, and it has eight bright
green rocking chairs with deerskin bottoms. The cots are
lined up like prone bodies under the windows of the bedrooms, and the rocking chairs seem to keep watch over
the river in front of the house. The porch is a marvelous
place for wet swimmers to lounge, and the dirt which
clings to bathing suits cannot hurt the furniture. In the
middle of the porch floor is a crack about two inches wide.
Dirt and sand are swept into this crack, and a pile of dirt
under the house is evidence of many years of living and
sweeping.

Behind the porch is the dining room, a very utilitarian
place about thirty feet long with a homemade table about
twenty feet long. Layers and layers of oilcloth cover the

table, and during family reunions I have seen twenty people sit down there and have plenty of room even for the elbows of people eating corn on the cob. A long bench stands between the table and the wall, and cane-bottomed chairs stand on the other side of the table. Grandmother's ancient refrigerator hums over all the talk, and always it quits running with a vigorous shake of its shoulders. On cold winter days my grandfather builds a roaring fire in the dining room fireplace, which is wide enough to burn a log five feet long. Sometimes a log which is a little wet will hiss and spew in the fire, and to me there is no more comfortable sound in the world than that.

Bluffton House means people. My grandparents have eight children, and there is almost never a day when some children and grandchildren do not come home for a visit. Once one daughter wrote from the city that she was coming for a visit and bringing her four children. Grandmother wrote a letter explaining that she could not come because workmen were painting the rooms and tiling the floors, but Grandfather asked her to tear up the letter and to send a warm invitation. They have an old radio, and sometimes they listen to the news. It is not a world for television and not for many books. Much of the family pleasure is talk. When several children and grandchildren visit at the same time, all of them seem to talk at once. Not many seem to listen, but somehow all the family stories do get heard along with the laughter and the babies crying and the shouts of children playing with strange old toys.

Everyone needs at least one good place in his life to love, and Bluffton is that place for me. It stands happy, comfortable, and enduring even in my dreams.

METAMORPHOSIS OF THE CAMPUS RADICAL

I am a born, habitual New Yorker and nothing surprises me more than to be living in Iowa, unless it is that as a former Ivy Leaguer and editor, I am now a teacher at the University of Iowa. Iowa City is Grant Wood's town, surrounded by his cornfields and cluttered with the American-Gothic houses which the Eastern eye takes some months to find appealing.

On the street you see an occasional bonneted Amish woman, in town for a visit to the dentist, or an occasional farmer making a deposit at the bank, but most of the people who pass, and smile, are university students. There are 20,000 here, attractive kids, many of the girls fair and fine-featured with the Scandinavian look of their farming forebears. The boys are of course bearded and long-haired, and the fashions of the times, overalls, boots, gold-rimmed spectacles, granny skirts and shawls, give the town the look of a period piece — everyone made up for a revival of "Oklahoma!"

The illusion of yesterday was shattered for me shortly after my arrival here two years ago. One midnight I saw crowds of students running through the streets to confront platoons of county police, spacemen in their helmets and plastic visors, and in the morning I stood looking into the smoking ruin of what had been the Rhetoric Building.

Now again, at the beginning of 1972, the feeling here as on other campuses is of relative serenity. Student steam has worked off in a political campaign that saw a favorite candidate elected to the City Council, and last year's window busters are busy with day-care centers and health-food cooperatives. The silence in town is such that casual observers size up the mood as a new campus apathy and suggest it is a return to the political indifference of the nineteen-fifties—but it is not that at all.

Most students maintain about the same enthusiasm for campus politics as for the fortunes of the chess team. Just as always, the preoccupation for a majority seems to be pleasure and, for a minority, scholarship. They are obsessive about it, grudgingly giving attention to social issues, and yet there is evidence of change in the last year or so, and of a new, homogenized sort of student.

For those few who do care about politics, the student body is a great sleeping beast which they are forever trying to prod awake. A bar and pizza joint which the student corporation opened this year is called The Hulk, after the fanciful Marvel Comics figure created by Stan Lee. He is a shambling brute, alter ego to Bruce Banner, a conscientious scientist. The Hulk is in fact a good-natured, gentle fellow, but when confused or misunderstood he is capable of a destructiveness that can be measured on a seismograph. The Hulk, the management explains, is the symbol of latent student power, not dimwitted exactly, but vulnerable and with a tendency to be misled.

There are two kinds of political students here—straight and radical. You cannot tell them apart by their look, which is stylish-hobo, nor their speech, which is reasonable and precise, although ridden with the drug-culture clichés. Neither likes things as they are, and there is general agreement on ends—a more humanized university, and power for themselves: power over people, the immediate environment and, ultimately, the nation. The disagreement is over means.

JOHN LEGGETT, in The New York Times Magazine

46i Use the following check list of essentials in writing themes.

Title

The title should accurately suggest the contents of the paper.

It should attract interest without being excessively novel or clever.

It should not be too long.

NOTE: Do not underline the title of your own paper (to represent italics), and do not put quotation marks around it.

Introduction

The introduction should be independent of the title. No pronoun or noun in the opening sentence should depend for meaning on the title.

It should catch the reader's attention.

It should properly establish the tone of the paper as serious, humorous, ironic, or otherwise.

It should include a thesis statement which declares the subject and the purpose directly but at the same time avoids worn patterns like "It is the purpose of this paper to . . . ."

It should be closely related to the main topic of the theme.

It should not be too long.

Body

The materials should develop the thesis statement.

The materials should be arranged in logical sequence.

Strong topic sentences (see §**45a**) should clearly indicate the direction in which the paper is moving and the relevance of the paragraphs to the thesis statement.

Technical terms should be explained.

Paragraphs should not be choppy.

Enough space should be devoted to main ideas. Minor ideas should be subordinated.

Concrete details should be used appropriately. Insignificant details should be omitted.

Transitions

The connections between sentences and those between paragraphs should be shown by good linking words. (See §**45e**.)

Conclusion

The conclusion should usually contain a final statement of the underlying idea, an overview of what the paper has demonstrated.

The conclusion may require a separate paragraph. But if the paper has reached significant conclusions all along, such a paragraph is not necessary for its own sake.

The conclusion should not merely restate the introduction.

Proofreading

Allow some time, if possible at least one day, between the last draft of the paper and the final finished copy. Then you can examine the paper objectively for wordiness, repetition, incorrect diction, misspellings, poor punctuation, choppy sentences, vague sentences, lack of transitions, and careless errors.

Subjects for Papers

A

Keep a notebook of items which you think may be useful to you as possible subjects and materials for papers.

B

Following are some suggested subjects.

Fewer Years for College
Old Photographs
Fair Journalism
Return to the Country
Political Cartoons
The New Music
Divorce
The New Freedoms
Blackness
Patterns of Humor
City Folklore
Walking
A Deserted House
Crime
Exploring
The Scientific Attitude
The Emergency Ward
Trip Down River

The Center City
Bad Teaching
Abortion
Television Commercials
An Ice Storm
Women's Equal Rights
The Average Man
Working in a Political Campaign
Good Fences and Good Friends
Educating the Parent
Camping Out
Parks
Censorship
The Subway at Night
Credit
Welfare
Acting in a Play
A Description of a Painting

C

The following quotations may help you to develop subjects for themes. Support, refute, exemplify, or use these quotations in any appropriate way. You may think of a subject only remotely related to what the author says.

1. "The older generation had certainly pretty well ruined this world before passing it on to us. They give us

this Thing, knocked to pieces, leaky, red-hot, threatening to blow up; and then they are surprised that we don't accept it with the same attitude of pretty, decorous enthusiasm with which they received it. . . ."

JOHN F. CARTER, JR., "The Overnight Realists"

2. "For the 15 per cent of adolescents who learn well in schools and are interested in subjects that are essentially academic, the present catch-all high schools are wasteful."

PAUL GOODMAN, "Freedom and Learning:
The Need for Choice"

3. "For generations we have tried to make the world a better place by providing more and more schooling, but so far the endeavor has failed."

IVAN ILLICH, "The Alternative to Schooling"

4. "Uncle Sam has become bankrupt when it comes to a conscience. . . ."

MALCOLM X, "The Black Revolution"

5. "The outstanding objection to the modern dance is that it is immodest and lacking in grace. It is not based on the natural and harmless instinct for rhythm, but on a craving for abnormal excitement."

THE HOBART COLLEGE *Herald*

6. "For there is a cloud on my horizon. A small dark cloud no bigger than my hand. Its name is Progress."

EDWARD ABBEY, *Desert Solitaire*

7. "The humor in *Peanuts*, then, has a dimension apart from the obvious gag level. This is because the characters in *Peanuts* are reflections of ourselves, and we are funnier than any make-believe character could possibly be."

MARTIN JEZER, "Quo Peanuts?"

8. "The American seems to be becoming more unable to demonstrate the individuality which democracy requires. Continuing hypnotism, emulsification, and homogenization of men by the media is the opposite of what our nation needs. . . ."

HARRY J. SKORNIA, "Ratings and Mass Values"

9. "The arts objectify subjective reality, and subjectify outward experience of nature. Art education is the education of feeling, and a society that neglects it gives itself up to formless emotion. Bad art is corruption of feeling."

SUSANNE K. LANGER, "The Cultural Importance of Art"

10. "The bad dreams of our Utopians will not come true; even the most complex, advanced thinking machine will not replace or dominate this [human] spirit."

JOHN H. TROLL, "The Thinking of Men and Machines"

11. "We are not so weak and timorous as to need to be free of fear; we need only use our capacity to not be afraid of it and so relegate fear to its proper perspective."

WILLIAM FAULKNER, "Faith or Fear"

12. "Religion will not regain its old power until it can face change in the same spirit as does science."

ALFRED NORTH WHITEHEAD, "Religion and Science"

13. "No great and enduring volume can ever be written on the flea, though many there be who have tried it."

HERMAN MELVILLE, *Moby-Dick*

14. "Whoso would be a man, must be a nonconformist."

RALPH WALDO EMERSON, "Self-Reliance"

15. "Stay, stay at home, my heart and rest;/Home-keeping hearts are happiest."

HENRY WADSWORTH LONGFELLOW

16. "A prophet is not without honor, save in his own country, and in his own house."

MATTHEW 13:57

17. "Home life as we understand it is no more natural to us than a cage is natural to a cockatoo."

GEORGE BERNARD SHAW, *Getting Married*

18. "To some extent a citizen of any country will feel that the tourist's view of his homeland is a false one."

MARY MCCARTHY, "America the Beautiful"

19. "Labor disgraces no man; unfortunately you occasionally find men disgrace labor."

ULYSSES S. GRANT, Speech at Birmingham, England

20. "The mass of men lead lives of quiet desperation. What is called resignation is confirmed desperation."

HENRY DAVID THOREAU, *Walden*

21. "Our life is frittered away by detail."

THOREAU, *Walden*

22. "Ah, one doesn't give up one's country any more than one gives up one's grandmother."

HENRY JAMES, *The Portrait of a Lady*

23. "Man's Unhappiness, as I construe, comes of his Greatness; it is because there is an Infinite in him, which with all his cunning he cannot quite bury under the Finite."

THOMAS CARLYLE, *Sartor Resartus*

24. "The mobs of great cities add just so much to the support of pure government, as sores do to the strength of the human body."

THOMAS JEFFERSON, *Notes on Virginia*

47 Writing About Literature

Any field of study has its own methods and its special vocabulary and terms. This section will explain briefly some of the techniques and problems in writing about literature.

47a Choose a precise topic and a meaningful title.

After you have selected a play, a short story, a novel, or a poem to write about, read it slowly, thoughtfully, and carefully. The good subject should come from the aspect of the work which causes the most precise and intense interaction between you and it. If you have thought long and well enough, you will probably find something that cries out for interpretation and comment. If the work does not cause that sort of reaction, you may need to choose another work if the assignment allows.

Select a subject appropriate to the length of the assignment. A narrow topic can be significant. Indeed, a short paper on the last paragraph in a novel could provide perspective on the entire novel and perhaps on the literary character of the author.

Give your paper a specific title which concisely but clearly announces your subject. A vague title like "A Criticism of Robert Frost's 'The Ax-Helve' " is virtually meaningless, too general because it does not name the paper's particular approach to the poem. A more exact title might be "Opposing Cultures in Frost's 'The Ax-Helve.' "

Although a paper may discuss several topics as they relate to the central point, a paper should have only one subject, one over-all argument to which every paragraph is related. Do not try to cover every aspect of a literary work. Provide focus.

47b Give your subject the appropriate kind of development.

The subject you choose will largely determine the way you write about it. The many kinds of writings about literature fall into several categories. Following are a few of the more significant ones with some remarks on special problems associated with each.

An Interpretation Most critical papers about literature result from a close study of the work. Several readings may be required. The writer of an interpretative paper is concerned with identifying themes and ideas. Through analyzing the techniques by which these are worked out, he is able to present specific evidence to support his interpretation. Be careful to distinguish between the thinking of a character and that of the author. Unless the author speaks for himself in his own person, you can only deduce from the work as a whole what he thinks.

A Review A good review should tell precisely what a work attempts to do and what methods it follows in carrying out its aim. If length permits, the review may include a brief outline of the contents. Such information should not be presented for its own sake, however, but as part of the attempt to give a fair and exact view of what the work accomplishes.

A Character Analysis Many students seize on the character sketch as an easy kind of critical paper to write. Actually it is a demanding assignment. The critic accomplishes little if he merely summarizes a character's traits and recounts his actions without considering motivation, development, and interrelationships with other characters. Alternatively, he may choose to describe the method of characterization—*how* the author makes the character what he is. Learn to distinguish between *character* and *characterization.*

A Study of Setting Often the time and place in which a work is set suggests something significant about the way places and things interact with people. If you choose to write about setting, you should be able to show how it is more than just a backdrop for the action.

A Comparative Study Much can be learned from comparing various facets of two or more works of literature. The purpose of the comparison is the crucial point here. To develop a comparison you must do more than discuss each work in turn. Many good comparative studies use one work to assist in the interpretation of another. Some comparisons reach conclusions that are more general. Two poems might be compared, for example, in such a fashion that the critic can then explain two ways in which poets create images.

Technical Analysis The analysis of technical elements in literature—imagery, symbolism, structure, prosody, and so on—requires special study of the technical term or concept as well as of the literary work itself. You might begin by consulting a good basic reference book like C. Hugh Holman, *A Handbook to Literature*, or M. H. Abrams, *A Glossary of Literary Terms*. Never use technical terms as labels for their own sake. Use them to help you identify and explain the distinctive literary quality of a work.

Some papers combine different kinds of approaches. A thoughtful paper on imagery, for example, does more than merely point out the images, or even the kinds of images, in the work under study. Rather it uses the imagery to interpret or analyze or clarify something else also—theme, structure, characterization, mood, relationships and patterns.

47c Do not summarize and paraphrase excessively.

Tell only as much of the story as you need to clarify your interpretations and to prove your arguments. Summarizing a plot does not involve much thinking, and the thought of a paper about literature is its crucial test.

47d Provide sufficient evidence.

Do not write too generally. A fundamental point in the evaluation of any paper is whether it strikes a proper balance between generalization and proof. Make a point; cite or quote a brief passage; show how it supports your point. Do not quote a long passage and expect your reader to analyze it for himself.

Your writing should say something significant both to a reader who knows the work intimately and to one who knows it only casually or not at all.

47e Think for yourself.

The excellence of your paper will depend finally on the significance of your thinking, your opinion. Do not merely report something you learned *from* the literature; write something you learned *about* it. Spend little or no time telling your reader that it is your belief; it is understood that opinions expressed are your own. Your readers will determine for themselves the importance of your paper, of your thinking, according to your accuracy, your evidence, your methods, your logic. Wild and unsupported thoughts are perhaps worse than pure summary or paraphrase, worse than no thinking at all.

47f Write about the literature, not about yourself or your reading process.

You may be interested in the difference between what you saw in a work on a first reading as opposed to your insights after a second reading, but omit such irrelevant information in your paper. Only your final and considered views should be presented to the reader.

Generally avoid the first person pronouns *I* and *we*. Excessive concern with yourself detracts from what you say about literature and causes irrelevance and wordiness.

47g Organize and develop your paper according to significant ideas.

Write significant topic sentences which present important subdivisions of the main argument. Go from point to point, idea to idea. Do not begin several paragraphs with such mechanical expressions as "In the first stanza . . ." and "In the second stanza. . . ." Organization by the chronology of a work is usually, though not always, less successful than moving from one of your own ideas to another.

NOTE: Early in your paper provide such necessary information as the name of the author or the title of the literary work you are discussing. Do not rely on your own title to provide such information.

47h Read what other writers say about literature and acknowledge your sources.

In papers written after a study of other critics' writings, you need to state your contribution, the difference between what they have written and what you think. This statement should be made in close association with your thesis sentence.

For bibliographies of writings about literature, see p. 265. For information about documentation and plagiarism, see §§ 48f and 48g.

Usually it is weak to begin a paper with a critic's name or idea. Establish your own subject and argument first.

Model Paper

Read the following poem by Allen Tate carefully, and
then read the student's critical paper which follows it.

THE TROUT MAP

The Management Area of Cherokee
National Forest, interested in fish,
Has mapped Tellico and Bald Rivers
And North River, with the tributaries
Brookshire Branch and Sugar Cove Creek:
A fishy map for facile fishery

In Marvel's kind Ocean*: drawn in two
Colors, blue and red-blue for the hue
Of Europe (Tennessee water is green),
Red lines by blue streams to warn
The fancy-fishmen from protected fish;
Black borders hold the Area in a cracked dish,

While other blacks, the dots and dashes, wire
The fisher's will through classic laurel
Over boar tracks to creamy pot-holes lying
Under Bald falls that thump the shying
Trout: we flew Professor, the Hackles and Worms.
(Tom Bagley and I were dotted and dashed wills.)

Up Green Cove gap from Preacher Millsap's cabin
We walked a confident hour of victory,
Sloped to the west on a trail that led us
To Bald River where map and scene were one

---

*An allusion to Andrew Marvell's "The Garden," in which he describes the
mind as "that ocean where each kind/Does straight its own resemblance
find. . . ." Marvell refers to the belief that every earthly creature is like a
similar ocean creature. Likewise, the mind contains counterparts to all
earthly beings.

In seen-identity. Eight trout is the story
In three miles. We came to a rock-bridge

On which the road went left around a hill,
The river, right, tumbled into a cove;
But the map dashed the road along the stream
And we dotted man's fishiest enthymeme
With jellied feet upon understanding love
Of what eyes see not, that nourished the will:

We were fishers, weren't we? And tried to fish
The egoed belly's dry cartograph —
Which made the government fish lie down and laugh.
(Tommy and I listened, we heard them shake
Mountain and cove because the map was fake.)
After eighteen miles our feet were clownish,

Then darkness took us into wheezing straits
Where coarse Magellan idling with his fates
Ran with the gulls for map around the Horn,
Or wheresoever the mind with tidy scorn
Revisits the world upon a dry sunbeam.
Now mapless the mountains were a dream.

Study the following interpretative paper carefully.
Identify the major points. Notice especially in the second
paragraph how the writer brings together his thinking
and brief quoted details which show how what he said
about the poem is true.

MAN AND NATURE IN ALLEN TATE'S "THE TROUT MAP"

Civilization has been in part the record of man's attempt to make contrivances which will enable him to deal with nature, but many of man's products fail rather than succeed. Allen Tate's poem "The Trout Map" describes man's relationship with nature during a fishing trip and the failure of a map to represent nature accurately. The men lose their way because of errors in the map, which represents man's rational attitude toward nature. The fish, the stream, and the other natural things defy man's attempts to know them and map them out.

Always the poem describes the map with contempt. It is a "fishy map for facile fishery"--fishy because it is supposed to show where the fish are and fishy too because it is unreliable, suspicious. The colors on the map are not really nature's colors. "Tennessee water is green," but the lines indicating streams on the map are blue. The color red warns against catching fish "protected" and probably stocked by the government for "fancy-fishmen." The boundary lines of black are unliving and they attempt to possess nature ("hold the Area"). They depict the shape of the forest as a man-made thing, a "cracked dish." The map leads men to the wilderness in mechanical fashion. The black dots and dashes indicating trails on the map do not guide the fishermen; they "wire" their wills

This paper is a revised version of a student paper originally written by Ralph Byers.

through the area. Three times the poet uses the image of dots and
dashes to show the great difference between marks on the map and the
actual trail, between man and nature.

The map at first seems to do its job well: they catch eight
trout in three miles. The map and the scene appear to be "one in
seen-identity." But then the "dry cartograph" becomes "man's
fishiest enthymeme." An enthymeme is a term in formal logic for a
syllogism in which one of the propositions is understood or assumed.
The syllogism of the map could be completed and stated as follows:
Maps help one to find one's way. The fishermen have a map. The
fishermen can find their way. But the enthymeme is fishy; the map
is wrong. The fishermen get lost, and even "the government fish
lie down and laugh." The map only appears to give structure to the
unstructured. It tries to reduce wildness and beauty to lines on a
piece of paper.

Many poetic devices in the poem contrast the wonders of nature
and man's coldly mechanical world. The very names of the first
stanza--"Tellico and Bald Rivers" and "Sugarcove Creek"--suggest an
unspoiled and frontier world. The laurel is "classic," a word which
probably means perfect and beautiful. The tracks of the wild hogs,
the stream's "creamy pot-holes," and the "shying trout" are aspects
of nature not shown on man's piece of paper. Other images, especially
of the streams, show how nature's energies are still powerful and
uncontrolled by man. The falls of the river "thump" the trout, and

later the stream leaves the road and tumbles "into a cove," a place away from the roads and the fishermen.

The men regard the map with an almost religious admiration. They follow it "upon understanding love / Of what eyes see not, that nourishes the will. . . ." They worship intelligence and scientific thought. Their arrogance and pathos are summed up in the line "We were fishers, weren't we?" Then the men, lost and laughed at by the fish, discover that the map is a fake. It is a fake because it is incorrect and also because it is based on a false sense of values and a false perception of nature.

At the end of the poem the fishing trip is over, but the poet continues to meditate on maps and their meaning. Magellan was coarse, but he knew how to live with nature. During his voyage around Cape Horn his maps were gulls, accurate representations of the natural world because they are a part of it. The last line, "Now mapless the mountains were a dream," can be read in two ways. Without the map the mountains seem like a vague dream to a man who has no label for them and consequently cannot envision their reality. In another sense, without the map the mountains are a dream in that they are mysterious and beautiful. That is the kind of dream the mountains are when man approaches nature on its terms and not his, when he gives up his rationality for something larger and greater than himself.

48 Writing the Investigative Paper

The investigative paper is based on a systematic search for information and conclusions, generally derived from materials found in a library. This section provides instructions about the way to assemble materials from sources and to document them with formal footnotes.

48a Choose a subject that interests you, and limit it to manageable size.

Your subject should allow you to use the library extensively, think for yourself, and come to a conclusion which will be of interest to your reader. Above all, it should really engage your attention so that you enjoy reading and thinking about it and writing it up for others.

Begin by choosing a general subject area. If you have long had a particular interest, it may be your starting point: photography, perhaps; or literature; or painting; or Africa. If nothing comes immediately to mind, start with a list of broad areas, such as the following, decide which one interests you most, and then focus on a limited sector of it.

the arts	government	industry
literature	sociology	science
philosophy	anthropology	technology
history	economics	medicine
religion	business	agriculture

At this stage you are concerned with relating your investigation to an active interest. Once you have done that, you are ready to narrow your subject down to manageable size.

Limit your subject. Make sure you can cover your subject in the assigned length of your paper. Suppose you have chosen photography as your general subject. After a little thought and reading and a look at the card catalog of the library, you will see that this is too broad a topic for one paper. So you may begin by limiting it to color photography, or aerial photography, or the history of photography. Any of these topics could be further limited: for example, "The Effect of Color Photography on Advertising," or "Aerial Photography in World War II," or "Matthew Brady: Photographer of the Civil War." Still further limitation may be desirable, depending on the length of your paper and the resources of your library.

If you are starting with an even broader area such as anthropology, history, science, or literature, you may move gradually toward your final subject by some such process as the following:

Anthropology—tribal societies—a tribal people still surviving—American Indians—the Navajo—the lore of the Navajo—Navajo songs.

Science—a study of science in some historical period—biology—evolution—evolution before Darwin—reactions to evolution in popular periodicals before Darwin.

Literature—the supernatural in literature—science fiction—tales of horror—famous monsters—*Frankenstein.*

In practice, narrowing down from a general to a specific subject is seldom smooth and orderly. Glean ideas for limiting a broad area by skimming an article in an encyclopedia or the subject headings in the card catalog. You may even be well into your preliminary research (see §48b) before you arrive at the final subject.

As you read and work, consider whether you are trying to cover too much ground or whether, at the other extreme, you are too narrowly confined. If you are not satisfied with your subject after you get into your preliminary reading, try with your instructor's help to work out an acceptable modification of it instead of changing your topic completely.

Avoid inappropriate subjects. Be wary of subjects highly technical, learned, or specialized. Only a specialist can handle modern techniques in genetic research or experimental psychology. Avoid topics that do not lead to a wide range of source materials. If you find that you are using one or two sources exclusively, the fault may be with your method—or with your topic. For example, a process topic (how to do something) does not lend itself to library investigation. Instead of writing on "How to Ski," the student might harness his interest in skiing to a study of the effect of skiing on some industry or region in the United States.

48b Become acquainted with the reference tools of the library, and use them to compile a working bibliography.

Certain guides to knowledge are indispensable to library investigation. From them you can compile a working **bibliography,** a list of publications which contain material on your subject and which you plan to read. The items on this list should have only the author's name, the title, and the information you need in order to find the source in the library.

Subject Card

Subject (usually in red)

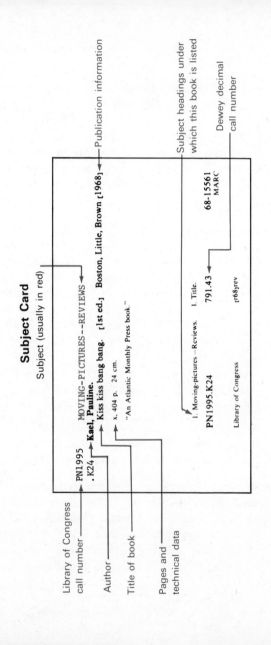

Library of Congress call number → PN1995 .K24

MOVING-PICTURES--REVIEWS ← Publication information

Author → Kael, Pauline.

Kiss kiss bang bang. [1st ed.] Boston, Little, Brown [1968]

Title of book → x, 404 p. 24 cm.

"An Atlantic Monthly Press book."

Pages and technical data

Subject headings under which this book is listed →

1. Moving-pictures—Reviews. 1. Title.

PN1995.K24   791.43 ← Dewey decimal call number

[r68]rev

68-15561
MARC

Library of Congress

Author Card

PN1995
.K24

Kael, Pauline.
 Kiss kiss bang bang. [1st ed.] Boston, Little, Brown [1968]

 x, 404 p. 24 cm.

 "An Atlantic Monthly Press book."

1. Moving-pictures — Reviews.   I. Title.

Title Card

Kiss kiss bang bang

PN1995
.K24
 Kael, Pauline.
 Kiss kiss bang bang. [1st ed.] Boston, Little, Brown [1968]

 x, 404 p. 24 cm.

 "An Atlantic Monthly Press book."

1. Moving-pictures — Reviews.   I. Title.

PN1995.K24   791.43   68-15561
                                               MARC

Library of Congress   [r68]rev.

The basic tool for finding books in the library is the **card catalog.** Here books are listed alphabetically by author and title. The card catalog also provides helpful subject headings, subheadings, and cross references which will lead you to new aspects of your topics. Reproduced on pages 260–261 are three typical catalog cards—actually three copies of the same Library of Congress card filed for three different uses. Notice the typed title and subject headings.

The card catalog leads you to the books in your library. The periodicals are indexed in special reference books, which list articles by author, title, and subject. The following periodical indexes are the most useful.

Periodical Indexes

Social Sciences and Humanities Index, 1965–. Formerly *International Index,* 1907–1965.
> Author and subject index to a selection of scholarly journals.

Readers' Guide to Periodical Literature, 1900–.
> An index to the most widely circulated American periodicals.

Biography Index, 1946–.
> "A Cumulative Index to Biographical Material in Books and Magazines."

Poole's Index to Periodical Literature, 1802–1906.
> An index by subject to the leading British and American periodicals of the nineteenth century.

Nineteenth Century Readers' Guide to Periodical Literature, 1890–1899.
> Author and subject index to some fifty English language general periodicals of the last decade of the nineteenth century.

The Art Index, 1929–.
> "A Cumulative Author and Subject Index to a Selected List of Fine Arts Periodicals."

The Music Index, 1949–.
> An index by author and subject to a comprehensive list of music periodicals published throughout the world.

Essay and General Literature Index, 1900–.
> "An Index to . . . Volumes of Collections of Essays and Miscellaneous Works."

The Dramatic Index, 1909–1949.
> "Covering Articles and Illustrations Concerning the Stage and Its Players in the Periodicals of America and England and Including the Dramatic Books of the Year."

The New York Times Index, 1913–.
> "The Master-Key to the News since 1851."

Subject Index to Periodicals, 1915–1922, 1926–1961.
> Superseded in part by *British Humanities Index*, 1962–. A subject index to a comprehensive list of British periodicals.

Public Affairs Information Service. *Bulletin*, 1915–.
> Subject index to periodicals and government publications chiefly in the social sciences.

Education Index, 1929–.
> "A Cumulative Subject Index to a Selected List of Educational Periodicals, Proceedings, and Yearbooks."

Agricultural Index, 1919–1964. Continued as *Biological and Agricultural Index*, 1964–.
> "A Cumulative Subject Index to Periodicals in the Fields of Biology, Agriculture, and Related Sciences."

The Industrial Arts Index, 1913–1957.
> In 1958 divided into the *Applied Science and Technology Index* and the *Business Periodicals Index*.
> "Subject Index to a Selected List of Engineering, Trade and Business Periodicals."

Business Periodicals Index, 1958–.
> A cumulative subject index to periodicals in all fields of business and industry.

Applied Science and Technology Index, 1958–.
> A cumulative subject index to a selection of English and American periodicals in such fields as aeronautics, automation, chemistry, electricity, engineering, physics.

Suppose you are writing on Mary Shelley's novel *Frankenstein*. Looking under *Shelley, Mary Wollstonecraft (Godwin)* in the *Social Sciences & Humanities Index*, volume nineteen, April 1965 to March 1966, you find the following entry:

SHELLEY, Mary Wollstonecraft (Godwin)
Frankenstein, or the new Prometheus. H.
Bloom. Partisan R 32:611–18 Fall '68

Subject heading
Title of article
Author of article
Abbreviation of the name of the
  periodical in which the article
  appears. Learn the complete
  name by checking inside the
  front cover of the periodical
  index.
Volume number
Pages
Date

With this information, you should be able to find the article if the periodical is in your library. Of course, you will be unable to read through all the articles written about a broad subject. But you will be able to exclude some merely by studying their titles in the periodical indexes.

Besides using the card catalog and the periodical indexes, you will need to know about several **general reference aids.** Many of these will give you bibliographical listings as well as surveys of your subject.

General Reference Aids

Articles on American Literature, 1900 – 1950; and *1950 – 1967.*

The Book Review Digest, 1905 –.

Cambridge Histories: Ancient, 12 vols.; Medieval, 8 vols.; Modern, 13 vols.

The Cambridge Bibliography of English Literature, 1941 – 1957. 5 vols.

New Cambridge Bibliography of English Literature, 1969 –.

Contemporary Authors, 1962 –.

Current Biography, 1940 –. "Who's News and Why."

Dictionary of American Biography 1928 – 1958. 22 vols.

Dictionary of National Biography, 1885 – 1949. 63 vols. and 10 supplementary vols. British.

Encyclopaedia Britannica. Supplemented by *Britannica Book of the Year, 1938 –.*

Encyclopaedia of Religion and Ethics, 1908 – 1927. 13 vols.

The Encyclopedia Americana. Supplemented by *American Annual, 1923 –.*

Encyclopaedia of the Arts, 1966.

Encyclopedia of Education, 1971. 10 vols.

The Encyclopedia of Philosophy, 1967. 8 vols.

Encyclopedia of Poetry and Poetics, 1965.

Encyclopedia of World Art, 1959 – 1968. 15 vols.

Grove's Dictionary of Music and Musicians. Fifth edition, 1954. 9 vols. Supplementary volume, 1961.

International Encyclopedia of the Social Sciences, 1968. 16 vols.

Literary History of the United States, 1963. 2 vols. (II, Bibliog.)

MLA International Bibliography of Books and Articles on the Modern Languages and Literatures, 1919 –.

McGraw-Hill Encyclopedia of Science and Technology, 1960. Third edition, 1971. 15 vols. Supplemented by *McGraw-Hill Yearbook of Science and Technology.*

The Mythology of All Races, 1916 – 1932. 13 vols.

The New Century Cyclopedia of Names, 1954. 3 vols.

Oxford History of English Literature, 1945 –.

Check your card catalog for special reference works in the area of your subject.

Your working bibliography should grow as you proceed. Be sure to include all the information that will help you find each item listed: along with the author and title, you will need the library call number for books, and the date, volume, and page numbers for articles.

48c **In your thinking and your writing, distinguish between primary and secondary materials.**

Primary materials are such things as a painting, a poem, a short story, a motor, a stock exchange, an animal, a fossil, a virus, or a public opinion poll. In a paper on gasolines, for example, the gasolines tested are primary materials; the writings of engineers about them are secondary. Primary materials for a study of tourists abroad would consist of published and unpublished diaries, journals, and letters by tourists, interviews of tourists, anything that was part of the tourist's life. Select a topic which allows use of primary materials so that you can reach independent conclusions and not rely entirely on the thinking of others.

Secondary materials are those written *about* your topic. In a study of tourists abroad, for examples, the writings of journalists and historians about them are called secondary sources. The significance and accuracy of such materials should be evaluated. It is important to consider when a work was written, what information was available to its author at that time, his general scholarly reputation, the extent of his knowledge and reliability as indicated in his preface or footnotes or bibliography, the logic he has demonstrated in proving his points, and even the medium of publication. A general article in a popular magazine, for example, is likely to be less reliable than a scholarly article in a learned journal.

48d Locate your source materials, read, evaluate, and take notes.

Before you begin to take notes, it is a good idea to do some broad **preliminary reading** on your subject in an encyclopedia or in other general introductory works. Try to get a general view, a kind of map of the territory within which you will be working.

After you have compiled a working bibliography (§ **48b**), located some of the sources you wish to use, and done some preliminary reading, you are ready to begin collecting specific material for your paper. If you are writing a formally documented paper, make a **bibliography card** for each item in your preliminary bibliography as you examine it. This will be a full and exact record of bibliographical information, preferably on a 3″ × 5″ filing card. From these cards you will later compile a bibliography to go at the end of your paper. A sample card is shown on p. 268. The essential information includes the name of the author, the title of the work, the place and date of publication, and the name of the publisher. If the work has an editor or a translator, is in more than one volume, or is part of a series, these facts should be included. Finally, record the library call number.

Having made the bibliography card, you are ready to read and take notes. For **note-taking**, use cards or slips of paper uniform in size. Cards are easier to use than slips, and they withstand more handling. Develop the knack of skimming so that you can move quickly over irrelevant

Bibliography Card

(reduced facsimile — actual size 3″ × 5″)

Author's name ———————→ Ritchie, Elizabeth

Title ———————→ Mary Shelley: Author of "Frankenstein"

Place of
publication and ———————→ New Brunswick: Rutgers Univ. Press
name of publisher

Date of
publication ———————→ 1953

Call number ———————→ PR 5398
                      N5

Bibliography

A label which indicates that this is a bibliography card. Keep these cards separate from those on which you take notes. They will eventually be the bibliography for your paper.

material and concentrate on pertinent information. Use the table of contents, the section headings, and the index to find chapters or pages of particular use to you in a book. As you read and take notes, consider what subtopics you will use. The two processes work together: your reading will give you ideas for subtopics, and the subtopics will give direction to your note-taking. At this point you are already in the process of organizing and outlining the paper. Suppose you wish to make a study of Mary Shelley's novel *Frankenstein*. You might work up the following list of tentative topics:

Mary Shelley's background
Stage and film versions of *Frankenstein*
Modern concept of the term "Frankenstein"
Mary Shelley's social philosophy
Frankenstein's tragic flaw
The quality of horror in *Frankenstein*

These headings may not be final. You should always be ready to delete, add, and change headings as you read and take notes. At this stage, the final order of headings—the outline—may be neither possible nor necessary.

To illustrate the methods of note-taking, suppose you have found the following paragraph about Mary Shelley.

Mary had been well trained in liberal thought. She had been brought up in the household of the author of *Political Justice;* she had elected at seventeen to become the "affectionate companion" of Shelley. She had early imbibed ideas of the superfluousness, in a reasonable and benevolent society, of positive institutions. When the many were great and good, there would result an ideal world whose foundations would be political freedom and a social order based on equality and justice.[1]

---

[1]Elizabeth Nitchie, *Mary Shelley: Author of "Frankenstein"* (New Brunswick: Rutgers Univ. Press, 1953), p. 35.

Paraphrased Notes

(reduced facsimile — actual size 3" × 5")

Subject heading ——————→ Mary Shelley's social thought

Identification of source.
Full bibliographical
information has been
taken down on the
bibliography card. ——————→ Ritchie, *Mary Shelley*

Page number ——————→ 35 Mary Shelley, largely because of her family
background, believed that social institutions
would be unnecessary when men accepted
each other benevolently and equally.

You may make a note on this passage by paraphrasing, by quoting, or by combining short quotations with paraphrasing.

To paraphrase is to express the sense of a passage entirely in your own words, selecting and summarizing only information and ideas that will be useful. The card opposite identifies the source, gives a subject heading, indicates the page number, and then records relevant information in the student's own words. It *extracts* items of information instead of merely recasting the entire passage and line of thought in different words. Notice the careful selection of details and the fact that the paraphrase is considerably shorter than the original.

If at the time of taking notes you cannot yet determine just what information you wish to extract, you may copy an entire passage. For later reference you must then be careful to show by quotation marks that it is copied verbatim.

A photoduplication machine, such as Xerox, can guarantee accuracy and save you time. At an early stage in research it is impossible always to know exactly what information is needed. Make a duplicate of some of the longest passages, and then you can study them and digest them during the writing of the first draft of the paper. Do not make so many copies that you leave too much of the thinking until the last moment, but use enough duplicates to prevent constant returns to the same books in the library.

When writing your paper, you may either quote directly or paraphrase. Except for the ellipsis, the following note went directly from book to card. (See §28c.)

> Mary Shelley's social thought
>
> Nitchie
>
> 35 "Mary had been well trained in liberal thought. She had been brought up in the household of the author of *Political Justice*.... She had early imbibed ideas of the superfluousness, in a reasonable and benevolent society, of positive institutions."

Short quotations and paraphrasing may be combined on a single note card, as in the following:

> Mary Shelley's social thought
>
> Nitchie
>
> 35 Mary Shelley was born into a family of liberal thinkers. Even when young she developed the idea of the "superfluousness, in a reasonable and benevolent society, of positive institutions."

It is most important to use quotation marks accurately when writing the note, to use your own words when not quoting, and to transfer quotations and quotation marks from card to paper with scrupulous care.

Any single card should contain notes from only one source, and all the notes on any single card should be about one single subject, such as Mary Shelley's social thought on the cards above. This will give you maximum flexibility in organizing materials when the plan of the paper takes shape. You will need to arrange the cards by topic before you write the paper.

The accuracy of your paper depends to a great extent on the accuracy of your notes. Indicate on each card the source, the page numbers, and an appropriate subject heading.

Note-taking is not a mere mechanical process; it involves interpretation and evaluation. Two persons writing on the same subject and using the same sources would not be likely to take quite the same notes, and their papers would differ accordingly in content and organization.

Study the following passage, which deals with the 1931 film about Frankenstein. Assume that you are writing a paper on that subject, and decide what kind of notes you would take.

> Florey was responsible for the plot twist whereby the Monster is given a madman's brain, hence betraying the author's original intention. Mary Shelley's tale tells of a scientist who creates a monster, a hideously misshapen creature, harmless at first but soon driven to commit murder and perform other acts of terror through the fear and revulsion his appearance provokes in others. The movie Monster is a murderous fiend, devoid (at least in this first appearance) of reason and barely glimpsed as human during the episode of the child who be-

friends him and whom he gratuitously drowns in a lake. This scene with the little girl, incidentally, was the only one to be deleted after audience reaction proved too violently adverse.[2]

From a passage as full of information as this one, it is possible to take several kinds of notes under different subject headings. Most of this material might eventually be used in a paper, but to a certain extent the student makes it his own by the way he selects and classifies it under his own subject headings. By the very process of reading and note-taking, he is thinking about his subject and organizing his thought. This is the supreme importance of taking notes, of quoting and paraphrasing. Now study the notes on pp. 275–276, all from the paragraph above. Observe the variety in subject headings and treatment.

48e Construct an outline.

As you read and take notes, think constantly about the organization of your paper. Revise subject headings, experiment with different ways of putting your topics and your notes in order, study your notes to detect gaps in evidence or weakesses in interpretation.

Your note cards should now be grouped by subject headings. Try to put the groups in the order in which you will present your material in your paper. You may shuffle the cards many times before you arrive at an order that satisfies you, and you may yet rearrange some topics during the process of writing.

See the model outline on page 289.

---

[2]Carlos Clarens, *An Illustrated History of the Horror Films* (New York: Putnam's, 1967), p. 63.

Quotation

The novel and the film

Clarens, <u>Horror</u> <u>Films</u>

63 "Florey was responsible for the plot twist
whereby the Monster is given a madman's
brain, hence betraying the author's original
intention.... the movie monster is a
murderous fiend, devoid...of reason and
barely glimpsed as human...."

Audience response to film

Clarens, <u>Horror</u> <u>Films</u>

63 "... the child who befriends him... he
[the Monster] gratuitously drowns in a lake.
This scene..., incidentally, was the only one
to be deleted after audience reaction proved
too violently adverse."

Paraphrase

Mary Shelley's Monster

Clarens, <u>Horror Films</u>

63 Unlike the film monster, the creature in Mary Shelley's novel is made to commit his violent acts because he is rejected by others.

Quotation and Paraphrase

Mary Shelley's Monster

Clarens, <u>Horror Films</u>

63 In the film "the Monster is given a madman's brain, hence betraying the author's original intention." In the novel the monster is "driven to commit murder" because others react to him with "fear and revulsion."

48f Acknowledge your sources. Avoid plagiarism.

Acknowledge your indebtedness to others by giving full details of sources in footnotes and bibliography. Using others' words and ideas as if they were your own is a kind of stealing called plagiarism.

Some of the principles of quoting and paraphrasing have already been discussed under the topic of taking notes (§ **48d**). These principles must be kept in mind during the writing and revision of the paper. Finally, quotations and paraphrases should be carefully checked for accuracy after the paper is written.

All direct quotations must be placed in quotation marks and acknowledged in your text. If you are writing a documented paper, specific details of the citation must be completed in a footnote (see pp. 279–283). Even when you take only a phrase or a single unusual word from a passage, you should enclose it in quotation marks. You may quote words, phrases, clauses, sentences, or even whole paragraphs. Generally you should quote a sentence or a paragraph only when a writer has phrased something especially well and when you need to give all the information he has given. Do not quote too much. A sequence of quotations strung together with a few words of your own is not satisfactory. Excessive quoting indicates that you have not properly digested your sources, thought about the ideas, and learned to express them in your own words and to relate them to your own ideas.

All paraphrases and citations must be acknowledged. Credit a source when you cite ideas or information from it even when you do not quote directly. Altering the wording does not make the substance yours. An acknowledgment not only gives proper credit but also lends authority to your statement. Whenever you consult a source or a note card as you write, you are probably paraphrasing, and you probably need an acknowledgment.

In paraphrasing you are expressing the ideas of another writer in your own words. A good paraphrase preserves the sense of the original, but not the form. It does not retain the sentence patterns and merely substitute synonyms for the original words, nor does it retain the original words and merely alter the sentence patterns. It is a genuine restatement. Invariably it should be briefer than the source. In the example below, notice the difference between a satisfactory and an unsatisfactory paraphrase:

ORIGINAL "Hemingway's debt to journalism was a large one, and he always acknowledged it. Unlike many ex-newspapermen, however, he neither sentimentalized the profession nor misunderstood its essential threat to creative writing."[3]

BADLY PARAPHRASED Hemingway's indebtedness to journalism was very great, and he himself said so. Unlike so many writers who have been newspaper men, however, he did not sentimentalize journalism or misunderstand that it is a danger to creative talent.

BETTER Hemingway admitted that he learned from newspaper work. But he also recognized that journalism can hurt a writer as well as help him.

If the source has stated the idea more concisely than you can, you should quote, not paraphrase.

Do not make use of extended paraphrases. If a good many of your paragraphs are simply long paraphrases,

---

[3]Charles A. Fenton, *The Apprenticeship of Ernest Hemingway* (New York: Farrar, 1954), p. 262.

your reader will assume that even your organization is taken from someone else. He will conclude that you have not assimilated your materials and thought independently about them—in short, that you have not done an acceptable piece of original work.

48g Follow accepted practices of documentation.

Although there is common agreement on the *principles* of documentation, the *forms* vary with almost every field, periodical, and publisher, and indeed every instructor. There are several good guides to documentation, but the most widely adopted style in language and literature is that recommended by the Modern Language Association of America in the *MLA Style Sheet.* The sample footnote and bibliographical entries listed below, as well as those in the model paper on pages 287–309, are based on the second edition of the *MLA Style Sheet.* The entries below may serve you as models, though your instructor may suggest or require modifications.

Sample Footnotes

Standard reference to a book
    ¹Charles Feidelson, Jr., *Symbolism and American Literature* (Chicago: Univ. of Chicago Press, 1953), p. 191.

Subsequent reference to a book
    ²Feidelson, p. 193.

NOTE: When two or more works by the same author have been cited previously, the new footnote should give the title or an abbreviated version of it:

    ³Feidelson, *Symbolism,* p. 111.

Standard reference to an article
⁴Richard Johnson, "Auden and the Art of Clarification," *Yale Review*, 61 (1972), 497.

NOTE: The abbreviation "p." is not used when the volume number is given. Inclusive page numbers for the article should be given in the bibliographical entry.

Standard reference to an article in a weekly or monthly magazine
⁵Alan Brien, "Take Me to Your Union Leader," *Punch*, 3 May 1972, p. 610.

NOTE: Page numbers in most weeklies and monthlies begin anew with each issue.

Subsequent reference to an article
⁶Johnson, p. 498.
⁷Brien, p. 612.

NOTE: See note for footnote 2 above.

Reference to a book by more than one author
⁸Walter R. Cuskey, Arnold William Klein, and William Krasner, *Drug-Trip Abroad: American Drug-Refugees in Amsterdam and London* (Philadelphia: Univ. of Pennsylvania Press, 1972), p. 90.

Reference to a book by more than three authors or editors
⁹Harvey A. Hornstein et al., eds., *Social Intervention: A Behavioral Science Approach* (New York: Free Press, 1971), p. 181.

NOTE: The Latin abbreviation "et al." (from *et alii*) means "and others."

Reference to a volume in a work of more than one volume
¹⁰George A. Simcox, *A History of Latin Literature from Ennius to Boethius* (New York: Harper, 1883), II, 438.

NOTE: The abbreviation "p." is not used when the volume number is given. In works where separate volumes have different publication dates, the volume number cited is given immediately after the title:

[11]Herbert M. Schueller and Robert L. Peters, eds., *The Letters of John Addington Symonds*, III (Detroit: Wayne State Univ. Press, 1969), 667. [Bibliographical entry gives inclusive dates of all volumes.]

Reference to an essay in a volume of essays

[12]Dorothy Emmet, "Coleridge and Philosophy," in *S. T. Coleridge*, ed. R. L. Brett (London: G. Bell, 1971), p. 210.

NOTE: Use the following form to refer to essays and articles reprinted in casebooks and other collections of essays:

[13]Alain Renoir, "Point of View and Design for Terror in *Beowulf*," *Neuphilologische Mitteilungen*, 63 (1962), rpt. in Donald K. Fry, ed., *The Beowulf Poet: A Collection of Critical Essays*, Twentieth Century Views (Englewood Cliffs, N.J.: Prentice-Hall, 1968), p. 156.

Reference to a book that is part of a series

[14]Edward Hubler, *The Sense of Shakespeare's Sonnets*, Princeton Studies in English, No. 33 (Princeton: Princeton Univ. Press, 1952), p. 117.

Reference to a second or later edition of a book

[15]Desmond King-Hele, *Shelley: His Thought and Work*, 2nd ed. (Teaneck, N.J.: Fairleigh Dickinson Univ. Press, 1971), p. 311.

NOTE: A modern reprinting of an older edition of a book is listed as follows:

[16]Edwin E. Slosson, *Major Prophets of To-Day* (1914; rpt. Freeport, N.Y.: Books for Libraries Press, 1968), p. 91.

Reference to a book with an editor

[17]Ann Radcliffe, *The Mysteries of Udolpho*, ed. Bonamy Dobrée (London: Oxford Univ. Press, 1966), p. 363.

Reference to an introduction to a book

[18]Bonamy Dobrée, "Introduction," Ann Radcliffe, *The Mysteries of Udolpho* (London: Oxford Univ. Press, 1966), pp. xv–xvi.

Reference to a book with a translator
     [19]Erich Maria Remarque, *Shadows in Paradise,* trans. Ralph Manheim (New York: Harcourt, 1972), p. 123.

Reference to a signed article in an encyclopedia
     [20]S[amson] L[ane] F[aison, Jr.], "Landscape Painting," *Encyclopaedia Britannica,* 1972.

NOTE: Authors with initials at the end of articles in encyclopedias can usually be identified by consulting the section (usually in the first volume) on contributors. Articles arrranged alphabetically in reference books do not need to be identified by volume and page.

Reference to an unsigned article in an encyclopedia
     [21]"Midway Islands," *Encyclopedia Americana,* 1964.

NOTE: A subsequent reference to this anonymous article could read simply:
     [22]"Midway Islands."

Reference to a newspaper article
     [23]"Churchill's Account of His Early Wars Is Ridiculed in a Contemporary's Notes," *New York Times,* 23 July 1972, sec. 1, p. 12, cols. 1–6.

NOTE: When an article is signed, the author's name should be given at the beginning of the footnote. When a newspaper issue has only one section, the section number, as given above, is not necessary.

Reference to a dissertation
     [24]James Thomas Jenkins, "A Theory of Magnetic Fluids," Diss. Johns Hopkins 1969, p. 72.

Biblical reference
     [25]I Kings iv.3. [Books of the Bible are not italicized.]

Reference to a play (with act, scene, and line)
     [26]*King Lear* v. iii. 245.

Reference to one author quoted in a book by another author
   [27]Ian Watt, *The Rise of the Novel* (Berkeley: Univ. of California Press, 1957), p. 125, quoted by Wayne C. Booth, *The Rhetoric of Fiction* (Chicago: Univ. of Chicago Press, 1961), p. 321.

Reference to an unsigned bulletin or pamphlet
   [28]*Enforcement of the Selective Service Law*, Special Monograph No. 14, Selective Service System (Washington, D.C.: GPO, 1951), pp. 102–103.

Reference to a signed bulletin or pamphlet
   [29]Charles E. Whieldon, Jr., and William E. Eckard, *West Virginia Oilfields Discovered before 1940*, Bulletin 607, Bureau of Mines, U.S. Dept. of the Interior (Washington, D.C.: GPO, 1963), p. 5.

Sample Bibliography

Booth, Wayne C. *The Rhetoric of Fiction*. Chicago: Univ. of Chicago Press, 1961.

Brien, Alan. "Take Me to Your Union Leader." *Punch*, 3 May 1972, pp. 610, 612.

"Churchill's Account of His Early Wars Is Ridiculed in a Contemporary's Notes." *New York Times*, 23 July 1972, sec. 1, p. 12, cols. 1–6.

Cuskey, Walter R., Arnold William Klein, and William Krasner. *Drug-Trip Abroad: American Drug-Refugees in Amsterdam and London*. Philadelphia: Univ. of Pennsylvania Press, 1972.

Dobrée, Bonamy. "Introduction." Ann Radcliffe, *The Mysteries of Udolpho*. London: Oxford Univ. Press, 1966.

Emmet, Dorothy. "Coleridge and Philosophy," in *S. T. Coleridge*. Ed. R. L. Brett. London: G. Bell, 1971, pp. 195–220.

Enforcement of the Selective Service Law. Special Monograph No. 14, Selective Service System. Washington, D.C.: GPO, 1951.

F[aison], S[amson] L[ane, Jr.] "Landscape Painting." *Encyclopaedia Britannica*, 1972.

Feidelson, Charles, Jr. *Symbolism and American Literature.* Chicago: Univ. of Chicago Press, 1953.

Hornstein, Harvey A., et al., eds. *Social Intervention: A Behavioral Science Approach.* New York: Free Press, 1971.

Hubler, Edward. *The Sense of Shakespeare's Sonnets.* Princeton Studies in English, No. 33. Princeton: Princeton Univ. Press, 1952.

Jenkins, James Thomas. "A Theory of Magnetic Fluids." Diss. Johns Hopkins, 1969.

Johnson, Richard. "Auden and the Art of Clarification." *Yale Review*, 61 (1972), 496–516.

King-Hele, Desmond. *Shelley: His Thought and Work.* 2nd ed. Teaneck, N.J.: Fairleigh Dickinson Univ. Press, 1971.

"Midway Islands." *Encyclopedia Americana*, 1964.

Remarque, Erich Maria. *Shadows in Paradise*, trans. Ralph Manheim. New York: Harcourt, 1972.

Renoir, Alain. "Point of View and Design for Terror in *Beowulf.*" *Neuphilologische Mitteilungen*, 63 (1962), rpt. in Donald K. Fry, ed., *The Beowulf Poet: A Collection of Critical Essays.* Twentieth Century Views. Englewood Cliffs, N.J.: Prentice-Hall, 1968, pp. 154–66.

Schueller, Herbert M., and Robert L. Peters, eds. *The Letters of John Addington Symonds.* 3 vols. Detroit: Wayne State Univ. Press, 1967–1969.

Simcox, George A. *A History of Latin Literature from Ennius to Boethius.* 2 vols. New York: Harper, 1883.

Slosson, Edwin E. *Major Prophets of To-Day.* 1914; rpt. Freeport, N.Y.: Books for Libraries Press, 1968.

Whieldon, Charles E., Jr., and William E. Eckard. *West Virginia Oilfields Discovered before 1940.* Bulletin 607, Bureau of Mines, U.S. Dept. of the Interior. Washington, D.C.: GPO, 1963.

Model Investigative Paper

A model investigative paper, with an outline and accompanying explanations, is given on the following pages for study.

Generally this paper follows the form outlined in the second edition of the *MLA Style Sheet*, with the following variations: footnotes are placed at the bottom of pages on which the references occur instead of being grouped in a separate section at the end of the paper; all blocked quotations are single-spaced; footnotes and bibliographical entries are single-spaced with double-spacing between them. These exceptions follow the conventional form for student papers. In these, as in other matters of form, follow the preference of your instructor.

Allow ample and even margins.
Double-space the text.
Indent five spaces for paragraphs.
Leave two spaces after periods and other terminal punctuation.
Leave one space after other marks of punctuation.

The material on the title page should be spaced so that it appears balanced on the page. Type the title in capital letters centered about one-third from the top of the page. Include your name and the name and section number of the course as indicated on the opposite page.

FRANKENSTEIN'S LONELY MONSTER

By

Anita Brooks

English 101
Section 1

If your instructor requests that you submit an outline with your paper, it should occupy a separate, unnumbered page following the title page and should follow the form for the topic outline illustrated in §46f, pp. 230–231.

OUTLINE

THESIS STATEMENT: An examination of Mary Shelley's <u>Frankenstein</u> reveals a novel with a strong moral and social theme, the need of human brotherhood.

I.   Versions of the story of Frankenstein

    A. The novel

    B. Later plays and motion pictures

    C. Common meaning of term "Frankenstein"

        1. Derivation of popular concept

        2. Difference between popular concept and theme of novel

II. Background of Mary Shelley's social thought

    A. Mary Wollstonecraft and women's rights

    B. William Godwin's social philosophy

III. Creation of monster and Frankenstein's response

    A. Monster's moral sense and early tendencies

    B. Frankenstein's revulsion

IV. Horror of loneliness

    A. Importance of loneliness as theme

    B. Robert Walton's search for companionship

    C. Monster's loneliness

        1. His plea for acceptance

        2. Nature of relationship with Frankenstein

        3. His grief over Frankenstein's death

    D. Frankenstein's isolation

V.   Frankenstein's tragic flaw

    A. His failure to love

    B. Mary Shelley's indictment of society

Type the title in capital letters and center it on the page. Triple-space between the title and the first line of text.

The first paragraph here provides exposition, information that the reader must have before he can understand the thesis statement and direction of the paper. After identifying the novel and the author, the paper tells how the adaptations of the original have created their own meanings of the scientist and the monster. Then in the last sentence of the paragraph, the paper gets back to the novel itself and provides direction and purpose with a strong thesis statement.

Place footnote numbers slightly above the line of type and after marks of punctuation. Do not leave a space before the number; do not place a period after the number. Number footnotes consecutively throughout the paper. Never repeat a number in the text even if the references are exactly the same.

Separate footnotes from the text by a short ruled line starting at the left-hand margin and placed far enough below the last line of the text so that it will not be mistaken for underlining to indicate italics.

Indent the first line of every footnote five spaces; do not indent succeeding lines.

In footnotes (but not in the bibliography) the author's name is written in normal order, first name first.

Footnote 1 shows how to refer to an article in a periodical and to a book. Note that the abbreviation "p." or "pp." is not used with the volume number.

Footnote 2 refers the interested reader to further material on the most famous film version of *Frankenstein*. Footnotes of this kind include information not directly relevant to the main subject of the paper, but closely enough related to warrant mention in a footnote. Note particularly the form of a reference to a periodical with each issue separately paginated.

The page number for the first page may be omitted or centered at the bottom.

FRANKENSTEIN'S LONELY MONSTER

Frankenstein, or the Modern Prometheus (1818) was written by nineteen-year-old Mary Wollstonecraft Shelley, the daughter of brilliant parents and the wife of a major poet, Percy Bysshe Shelley. Almost from the time of the novel's publication, Victor Frankenstein and his horrible monster have been the subjects of dozens of plays and, in the twentieth century, scores of motion pictures.[1] Most of them have two ingredients in common. They tend to make Victor Frankenstein a cold, inhuman scientist, and they portray the monster as a conscienceless, uncontrollable killer (with the diseased brain of a criminal), who grunts his way from one murder to another.[2] Mainly because of these popular and highly sensational versions of Mary Shelley's novel, "Frankenstein" has become a household word, "a synonym for a man whose own works bring him to disaster or destruction.

---

[1]For an excellent treatment of plays based on Mary Shelley's novel, see Elizabeth Nitchie, "The Stage History of Frankenstein," South Atlantic Quarterly, 41 (1942), 384-98. For information about motion pictures that portray Frankenstein and the monster, see Ivan Butler, The Horror Film (New York: A. S. Barnes, 1967), pp. 40-45.

[2]The most famous and influential of all motion pictures about Frankenstein was that which appeared in 1931 and starred Boris Karloff as the monster. When it appeared in December in New York, one reviewer commented that the monster communicated its anger and frustration by "squeaking and grunting." "Frankenstein," Time, 14 Dec. 1931, p. 25. For discussions of this film, see the following: Carlos Clarens, An Illustrated History of the Horror Films (New York: Putnam's, 1967), pp. 62-65; Raymond Durgnat, Films and Feelings (Cambridge, Mass.: M.I.T. Press, 1967), p. 106; and Pauline Kael, Kiss Kiss Bang Bang (Boston: Little, Brown, 1968), p. 148.

Place the page number in the upper right-hand corner, two lines above the first line of text. Use Arabic numerals; do not put a period after the number.

To place special emphasis upon these words, which will be used again later in the paper, the writer has underlined them. When this is done, the writer must indicate that his own emphasis has been added.

When an ellipsis is used to indicate omitted words at the end of a sentence, the three periods are accompanied by a fourth.

Footnote 3 illustrates the standard form for a signed article in an encyclopedia.

Footnotes are used not only to give the reader further references to read and to lead him to the sources used in the paper, but also to aid in developing the argument by giving evidence or example as footnote 5 illustrates.

Footnote 6 illustrates a reference to the editor's introduction to a work by another writer.

And as the monster . . . bears no name, the name of his creator has been often transferred to him so that 'a Frankenstein' has come to signify, in popular usage, a being of the most appalling ugliness and brutality, <u>having no trace of the moral sense whatever</u>" (italics mine).[3] This modern concept of Frankenstein and his monster differs widely from the original. An examination of Mary Shelley's novel reveals a book with a strong moral and social theme, the need of human brotherhood.

It was no accident that Mary Shelley should stress this social ideal in her first novel. She was nurtured on the principles of equality. Her mother, Mary Wollstonecraft Godwin, was a vigorous campaigner for women's rights.[4] Mrs. Godwin's most notable book, <u>A Vindication of the Rights of Woman</u> (1792), is a bold and brilliant plea for equality.[5] In it she "points out that among 'unequals there can be no society.' She insists on this condition of equality for all mankind. . . ."[6]

With even greater effectiveness, Mary Shelley's father, William Godwin, wrote about the need for a benevolent society that would allow

---

[3] Wilbur L. Cross, "Frankenstein," <u>Encyclopedia Americana</u>, 1964.

[4] See Ralph M. Wardle, <u>Mary Wollstonecraft: A Critical Biography</u> (Lawrence: Univ. of Kansas Press, 1951), and Elizabeth Robins Pennell, <u>Mary Wollstonecraft Godwin</u> (London: Allen, 1885).

[5] Mary Shelley did not know her mother, who died when Mary was born. However, she was well acquainted with Mary Godwin's writings and shared many of her ideas.

[6] Charles W. Hagelman, Jr., "Introduction," Mary Wollstonecraft, <u>A Vindication of the Rights of Woman</u> (New York: Norton, 1967), p. 16.

Notice that this paragraph contains information from four different sources. Basing an entire paragraph on one source is often a sign of inadequate research and thought.

Since "a trace of the moral sense" was quoted and documented on p. 2, a new footnote is not necessary here.

Quotations of more than two lines of poetry are generally set off as shown here. The writer has indicated in parentheses the book number and lines of the quotation from *Paradise Lost.* The punctuation mark at the end of a blocked quotation comes before, not after, the parenthesis.

Footnote 7 (Brailsford) illustrates a reference to a book which carries no copyright date.

Footnote 10 illustrates a reference to one volume in a multi-volumed work. The number of volumes in the collected work and the inclusive dates of publication are not given here but in the bibliographical entry. With the volume number, which is given in Roman numerals in a reference to a volume in a multivolumed work, the abbreviation "p." is not used with the page number. The abbreviation "et al." indicates that the work has more than three authors (or, in this case, editors).

every man his individual and equal place. He was one of the most
famous thinkers of his time and author of the celebrated _An Inquiry
Concerning the Principles of Political Justice_ (1793).[7] In that and
other works, including such novels as _Caleb Williams_ (1794), he showed
"vast faith in the individual's ability to develop his reason and
natural benevolence so that he could live peaceably and usefully with
other men."[8] It is not surprising, then, that _Frankenstein_ is among
other things a book with a definite social message, a theme that
follows in the tradition of Mary Shelley's famous mother and father.[9]

In the novel the monster does have "a trace of the moral sense."
Indeed, he is a creature of great sensitivity who suffers intensely.
The responsibility for this suffering lies squarely on the man who
created him. A creator always has an obligation to the thing he
creates. As an epigraph for _Frankenstein_, Mary Shelley chose the
following lines from Milton's _Paradise Lost_ that reflect the creature's
point of view:

> Did I request thee, Maker, from my clay
> To mould me Man? Did I sollicite thee
> From darkness to promote me . . . ? (X. 743-45)[10]

---

[7] See H. N. Brailsford, _Shelley, Godwin, and Their Circle_ (New
York: Holt, n.d.), and Elton Edward Smith and Esther Greenwell Smith,
William Godwin (New York: Twayne, 1965).

[8] David McCracken, "Introduction," William Godwin, _Caleb Williams_
(London: Oxford Univ. Press, 1970), p. viii.

[9] For a discussion of her parents' influence on Mary Shelley's
Frankenstein, see Mary Graham Lund, "Mary Godwin Shelley and the
Monster," _University of Kansas City Review_, 28 (1962), 253-58.

[10] _Paradise Lost_, ed. Frank Allen Patterson et al., II, pt. 2
(New York: Columbia Univ. Press, 1931), 331.

Note the proper way to place a footnote number after ellipsis and quotation marks at the end of a sentence.

Footnote 12 is the only footnote needed for page references to *Frankenstein.* Once the writer has indicated which text of the novel he is using, he may then place page numbers in the text where the quotations occur. Frequently the writer has a choice of which text of a novel or poem to use. He should investigate fully to determine the most reliable text, for texts sometimes vary. Scholarly articles have been based on passages in poems and novels which proved — with considerable embarrassment to the scholar — to be not what the author actually wrote. In the case illustrated here, scholars say both texts are reliable, but one is somewhat better than the other because it retains the epigraph which Mary Shelley included originally.

4

At his creation the monster is "a plain page on which could be written good or evil."[11] His original tendencies are toward love and unselfishness. Across this blank page of his mind, his creator immediately writes his rejection. Young Victor Frankenstein eagerly studies chemistry and physiology, patches together an eight-foot ogre with yellow complexion and watery eyes from the remains of charnel houses, fuses life into the creature through some process left mysterious in the novel, and then turns away in total disgust. His initial horror is not the result of any awareness that he has presumed to equal God. That awareness comes later. He rejects the monster simply because it is unbearably ugly: "Now that I had finished, the beauty of the dream vanished, and breathless horror and disgust filled my heart. Unable to endure the aspect of the being I had created, I rushed out of the room . . . ."[12]

Time and again Frankenstein, who tells his story to a young explorer named Robert Walton, returns to the monster's ugliness as the reason for his rejection of it: "Oh! no mortal could support the horror of that countenance. A mummy again endued with animation could not be so hideous as that wretch. I had gazed on him while unfinished; he was ugly then; but when those muscles and joints were

---

[11]Elizabeth Nitchie, Mary Shelley: Author of "Frankenstein" (New Brunswick: Rutgers Univ. Press, 1953), p. 34.

[12]Mary W. Shelley, Frankenstein, or the Modern Prometheus, ed. M. K. Joseph (London: Oxford Univ. Press, 1969), p. 57. All references are to this edition. This is a recent and reliable edition of the novel. The Everyman Edition (New York: Dutton, 1912) does not include the epigraph noted above.

Note the proper way to indicate a page number in parentheses at the end of a sentence. The period goes *outside* the parenthesis.

Prose quotations of less than 100 words should generally be run-on in the text. It is annoying and distracting to read a page where the writer has set off every quotation, no matter how brief.

Always be certain that no words are erroneously attributed to the source and that all words in the source are properly enclosed in quotation marks. Follow punctuation and capitalization of the source.

When prose quotations are over 100 words, they should be set off as indicated here. Indent five spaces and single-space within the quotation. Paragraphing within the passage should follow the source. Indent three additional spaces for new paragraphs. *Do not enclose blocked quotations in quotation marks.*

rendered capable of motion, it became a thing such as even Dante could not have conceived" (p. 58). In later encounters Frankenstein understandably feels hatred as well as horror, for the monster is engaged in killing Frankenstein's family and friends.

When the monster tells his side of the story, beginning about the middle of the novel, he stresses two feelings: his desperate need for love and his bitterness over his rejection by his creator (and by other men). It becomes clear that Mary Shelley has written a horror story in a deeper sense than the obvious, for _Frankenstein_ is centrally about the horror of loneliness. This theme comes to the surface early in the novel when Robert Walton, on his way to explore the North Pole, writes home to his sister: "I have one want which I have never yet been able to satisfy; and the absence of the object of which I now feel as a most severe evil. I have no friend, Margaret: when I am glowing with the enthusiasm of success, there will be none to participate my joy; if I am assailed by disappointment, no one will endeavour to sustain me in dejection" (p. 19).

Walton's complaint foreshadows the monster's pathetic and moving outcry to Frankenstein, whom he has followed into the wilds of the Alps, hoping for acceptance:

> How can I move thee? Will no entreaties cause thee to turn a favourable eye upon thy creature, who implores thy goodness and compassion? Believe me, Frankenstein: I was benevolent; my soul glowed with love and humanity: but am I not alone, miserably alone? You, my creator, abhor me; what hope can I gather from your fellow-creatures, who owe me nothing? they spurn and hate me. The desert mountains and dreary glaciers are my refuge. I have wandered here many days; the caves of ice, which I only do not fear, are a dwelling to me, and the only one which man does not grudge. These bleak skies I hail, for they are kinder to me

After a blocked quotation the page reference in parentheses comes *outside* (not inside as in the case of run-on quotations) the final period.

A new paragraph may or may not be necessary after a blocked quotation. Here the student continues her discussion of the monster's desire for acceptance and links it with the writing of Mary Shelley's mother.

Footnote 13 illustrates one form for referring to a work mentioned in a previous footnote (see footnote 6). The name of the work rather than the author is given because the first reference was to the editor's introduction. If it were the introduction rather than the book itself referred to here, the footnote would read "Hagelman" with the proper page number. The *MLA Style Sheet* gives the following advice about subsequent references: "Be brief. Be clear. Do not rely upon your reader's memory. In most cases, use the author's last name, followed by an intelligible short title, e. g., Wallerstein, *Crashaw*, p. 56. If only one work by a given author is referred to in your article, if the full reference is readily found in a recent note, and if no other writer with an identical surname is being cited, your author's surname, never abbreviated, suffices for the reference, e.g., 'Wallerstein, p. 56.' Always avoid repeating long titles. Avoid Latin reference tags; they rarely save space and can severely try your reader's patience."

Footnote 14 illustrates the standard form for referring to a work mentioned in a previous footnote.

than your fellow-beings. If the multitude of mankind knew of
my existence, they would do as you do, and arm themselves for
my destruction. (p. 100)

In this passage and others like it where the monster begs for social

acceptance, one can hear the echo of Mary Shelley's mother as she

pleaded for equality: "Would men but generously snap our chains, and

be content with rational fellowship instead of slavish obedience,

they would find us more observant daughters, more affectionate

sisters, more faithful wives, more reasonable mothers--in a word,

better citizens. We should then love them with true affection,

because we should learn to respect ourselves."[13] This section of

Frankenstein, where the monster recounts the agony he has suffered,

presents, as Mary Graham Lund has put it, "some of the most beautiful

and tender scenes in the novel. We see a good and innocent being

transformed into a brutal, vengeful monster because it is rejected by

society, thrust out into utter loneliness."[14]

   Although the bitterness that comes from loneliness drives the

monster to vengeful killings, he never gives up his love for Franken-

stein.[15] At the end, when Frankenstein has died of exhaustion in

chasing the creature across the icy wilderness of the far North,

Walton finds the monster on his ship grieving over the body of his

---

[13]Vindication, p. 224.

[14]Lund, p. 255.

[15]The monster kills Frankenstein's brother William in an early
rage at being rejected, but the later murders result from Frankenstein's going back on his promise to create a female creature to
alleviate the loneliness of the monster.

As a rule place page references at the end of a sentence. When a single sentence contains quotations from different pages, however, these pages should be given where they occur.

As illustrated here, quotations need not always be set apart in separate sentences. Frequently the flow of the argument is more graceful if quotations can be made a part of the writer's own sentences.

creator. Walton, who knows for himself the terrors of loneliness, is moved by the monster's words. As he speaks, it is clear that the modern concept of Frankenstein's monster as a creature that possesses "no trace of the moral sense whatever" bears little resemblance to Mary Shelley's creation. In his "exclamations of grief and horror" (p. 218), the monster addresses his dead creator: "Blasted as thou wert, my agony was still superior to thine; for the bitter sting of remorse will not cease to rankle in my wounds until death shall close them for ever" (p. 223). Again the monster returns to the causes of his evil--rejection and loneliness: "I cannot believe that I am the same creature whose thoughts were once filled with sublime and transcendent visions of the beauty and the majesty of goodness. But it is even so; the fallen angel becomes a malignant devil. Yet even that enemy of God and man had friends and associates in his desolation; I am alone" (p. 221). He succeeded in ruining Frankenstein's life, but now he feels only emptiness and remorse, and through it all, he says, "still I desired love and fellowship, and I was still spurned" (p. 221). As the novel ends the monster tears himself away from Frankenstein and strikes out alone, soon to set fire to himself and end his life.

Frankenstein's loneliness is also intense. After giving life to the creature, he feels alienated from all of humanity. He prefers to be by himself. He is a solitary figure, walking in the Alps, living amid the lonely Orkney Islands, or chasing the monster across the desolate ice. His guilt and later his obsession--which is to kill the monster--make it impossible for him to be a part of society. All three major characters, therefore, feel the terrible emptiness that

In the long quotation brackets have been used to indicate that the words "the monster" are not in the original text (see §**26**). Brackets are also used to enclose the abbreviation "sic" when a word in a quotation has been misspelled. This assures your reader that the misspelling is not yours and that you are quoting accurately. Note the following example: "Her mother, Mary Wollstonecroft [sic], who was from Dublin, wrote a treatise on the rights of woman. . . ." Robert Sencourt, "Mary Wollstonecroft [sic] Shelley," *Contemporary Review*, Oct. 1957, p. 215.

Although the quotation referred to in footnote 17 comes from the same volume as the quotations from *Frankenstein*, which are included in the text, a separate footnote is necessary because this reference is not to the novel proper but to its introduction by M. K. Joseph.

Footnote 19 illustrates that the name of the author of a work is not generally used in the footnote when his name has been mentioned in the text before the quotation.

comes from being cut off from human fellowship. The novel makes it plain that the knowledge which both Victor Frankenstein and the explorer Robert Walton seek after is not "a higher good than love or sympathy."[16]

If Frankenstein's creature had been treated with kindness and accepted into the brotherhood of man, loneliness would not have twisted his original benevolence into malignancy. As one critic argues: "The monster is essentially benevolent; but rejection by his creator and by mankind at large has made him first a fallen Adam and then a fallen Lucifer."[17] Percy Bysshe Shelley wrote perceptively of the theme of his wife's book:

> Nor are the crimes and malevolence of the single Being [the monster], though indeed withering and tremendous, the offspring of any unaccountable propensity to evil, but flow irresistibly from certain causes fully adequate to their production. They are the children, as it were, of Necessity and Human Nature. In this the direct moral of the book consists; and it is perhaps the most important, and of the most universal application, of any moral that can be enforced by example. Treat a person ill, and he will become wicked. Requite affection with scorn;--let one being be selected, for whatever cause, as the refuse of his kind-- divide him, a social being, from society, and you impose upon him the irresistible obligations--malevolence and selfishness.[18]

Frankenstein's error is, as Harold Bloom has stated, "his failure to love."[19] But it is not his shortcoming alone. Mary Shelley, who

---

[16]M. A. Goldberg, "Moral and Myth in Mrs. Shelley's *Frankenstein*," *Keats-Shelley Journal*, 8 (1959), 33.

[17]M. K. Joseph, "Introduction" to *Frankenstein*, p. xi.

[18]"On Frankenstein," *Prose Work*, ed. Roger Ingpen and Walter E. Peck, VI (New York: Scribner's, 1929), 264.

[19]"Frankenstein, or the New Prometheus," *Partisan Review*, 32 (1965), 614.

Footnote numbers should generally be placed at the end of a sentence. In the case of footnote 20, part of the sentence quotes a critic; the other part reflects the thought of the writer. Therefore to place the number at the end of the sentence would give the erroneous impression that the entire thought was the critic's.

The concluding paragraph sums up the argument of the paper. It is largely the writer's own thinking. Secondary sources can be made use of in the conclusion in a minor way, as here, but it is more effective not to make extensive use of them. Especially avoid beginning your paper and ending it with a quotation.

Footnote 20 includes the title *"Mary Shelley"* because the same author was referred to in footnote 1 as the author of another work. If footnote 20 had read simply "Nitchie," with a page number, the reader might not know if the writer meant to refer to the article mentioned in footnote 1 or to the book mentioned in footnote 11.

"had been well trained in liberal thought,"[20] indicted mankind for its lack of genuine benevolence, for its prejudice and selfishness. Frankenstein failed not merely because he presumed to equal God in the creation of another being, but because he could not follow through with the love and concern that a creator must have for his creature, that one man must have for another no matter how different they are. Intellectually he came close to being godly, but his heart remained that of an ordinary man, too small to take in anything as different and as ugly as the monster. Consequently, he created a thing far worse than his monster--the despair of loneliness.

---

[20]Nitchie, Mary Shelley, p. 35.

Start the bibliography on a new page as the last section of your paper. Head the page BIBLIOGRAPHY, in capital letters, centered. Triple-space below the heading.

Do not indent the first line of an entry; indent succeeding lines five spaces.

Double-space between entries; single-space within an entry.

List only those sources actually used in your paper and referred to in footnotes.

Authors are listed with surname first. If a book has more than one author, however, the names of authors after the first one are put in normal order.

List entries alphabetically. When more than one book by the same author is listed, use a long dash (about one inch) in place of the author's name in entries after the first. An entry without an author (for example, an unsigned magazine article) is listed alphabetically by the first word.

List the inclusive pages of articles.

Notice that the important divisions of entries are separated by periods.

A bibliographical entry should include all the information that will enable the reader to find the source readily if he wishes to do so.

10

BIBLIOGRAPHY

Bloom, Harold. "Frankenstein, or the New Prometheus." _Partisan Review_, 32 (1965), 611-18.

Brailsford, H. N. _Shelley, Godwin, and Their Circle_. New York: Holt, n.d.

Butler, Ivan. _The Horror Film_. New York: A. S. Barnes, 1967.

Clarens, Carlos. _An Illustrated History of the Horror Films_. New York: Putnam's, 1967.

Cross, Wilbur L. "Frankenstein." _Encyclopedia Americana_, 1964.

Durgnat, Raymond. _Films and Feelings_. Cambridge, Mass.: M.I.T. Press, 1967.

"Frankenstein." _Time_, 14 Dec. 1931, p. 25.

Godwin, William. _Caleb Williams_. Ed. David McCracken. London: Oxford Univ. Press, 1970.

Goldberg, M. A. "Moral and Myth in Mrs. Shelley's _Frankenstein_." _Keats-Shelley Journal_, 8 (1959), 27-38.

Kael, Pauline. _Kiss Kiss Bang Bang_. Boston: Little, Brown, 1968.

Lund, Mary Graham. "Mary Godwin Shelley and the Monster." _University of Kansas City Review_, 28 (1962), 253-58.

Milton, John. _The Works of John Milton_. 18 vols. Ed. Frank Allen Patterson et al. New York: Columbia Univ. Press, 1931-1938.

Nitchie, Elizabeth. _Mary Shelley: Author of "Frankenstein."_ New Brunswick: Rutgers Univ. Press, 1953.

_____. "The Stage History of _Frankenstein_." _South Atlantic Quarterly_, 41 (1942), 384-98.

Pennell, Elizabeth Robins. _Mary Wollstonecraft Godwin_. London: Allen, 1885.

Shelley, Mary Wollstonecraft. _Frankenstein, or the Modern Prometheus_. Ed. M. K. Joseph. London: Oxford Univ. Press, 1969.

Shelley, Percy Bysshe. _The Complete Works of Percy Bysshe Shelley_. 10 vols. Ed. Roger Ingpen and Walter E. Peck. New York: Scribner's, 1926-1930.

Smith, Elton Edward, and Esther Greenwell Smith. _William Godwin_. Twayne's English Authors Series. New York: Twayne, 1965.

Wardle, Ralph M. _Mary Wollstonecraft: A Critical Biography_. Lawrence: Univ. of Kansas Press, 1951.

Wollstonecraft, Mary. _A Vindication of the Rights of Woman_. Ed. Charles W. Hagelman, Jr. New York: Norton, 1967.

Glossary of Usage and Terms

Many items not listed here are covered in other sections of this book and may be located through the index. For words and terms found neither in this glossary nor in the index, consult an up-to-date dictionary. The usage labels (*informal, dialectal*, etc.) affixed to words in this glossary reflect the opinions of two or more of the dictionaries listed on page 147.

49 Glossary *g*

A, an Use *a* as an article before consonant sounds; use *an* before vowel sounds.

a nickname	an office
a house	an hour
(the *h* is sounded)	(the *h* is not sounded)
a historical novel	
(though the British say *an*)	
a union	an uncle
(long *u* has the consonant sound of *y*)	

Absolute phrase   See §20L.

Accept, except   As a verb, *accept* means *to receive; except* means *to exclude. Except* as a preposition also means *but.*

> Every legislator *except* Mr. Whelling refused to *accept* the bribe.
>
> We will *except* (i.e., exclude) this novel from the list of those to be read.

Accidently   A misspelling usually caused by mispronunciation. Use *accidentally.*

Ad   Informal; a clipped form of *advertisement.*

Adjective   A word which modifies a noun or a pronoun.

> *Her old* hound jumped over *that high* clothesline for *the third* time.

Adjective clause   See **Dependent clause.**

Adverb   A word which modifies a verb, an adjective, or another adverb.

> The surrendering general *very humbly* handed the captain his *rather* rusty sword.

See §10.

Adverbial clause   See **Dependent clause.**

Affect, effect   *Affect* is a verb meaning *to act upon* or *to influence. Effect* may be a verb or a noun. *Effect* as a verb means *to cause* or *to bring about; effect* as a noun means *a result, a consequence.*

> The patent medicine did not *affect* (influence) the disease.
>
> The operation did not *effect* (bring about) an improvement in his health.
>
> The drug had a drastic *effect* (consequence) on the speed of the patient's reactions.

Aggravate Informal in the sense of *annoy, irritate,* or *pester.* Formally, it means *to make worse or more severe.*

Agree to, agree with *Agree to* a thing (plan, proposal); *agree with* a person.

> He *agreed to* the insertion of the plank in the platform of the party.
>
> He *agreed with* the senator that the plank would not gain many votes.

Ain't Nonstandard or illiterate.

All ready, already *All ready* means *prepared, in a state of readiness; already* means *before some specified time* or *previously,* and describes an action that is completed.

> The hunters were *all ready* to take horse. (fully prepared)
>
> Mr. Bowman had *already* bagged his limit of quail. (action completed at time of statement)

All together, altogether *All together* describes a group as acting or existing collectively; *altogether* means *wholly, entirely.*

> The sprinters managed to start *all together.*
>
> I do not *altogether* approve the decision.

Allusion, illusion An *allusion* is a casual reference. An *illusion* is a false or misleading sight or impression.

Alright Not considered standard for *all right.*

A.M., P.M. Used only with figures, as in "6:00 P.M." Not to be used for *morning* or *afternoon* as in "The wreck occurred this P.M."

Among, between *Among* is used with three or more persons or things; *between* is used with only two.

> It will be hard to choose *between* the two candidates.
>
> It will be hard to choose *among* so many candidates.

Amount, number   *Amount* refers to mass or quantity; *number* refers to things which may be counted.

> That is a large *number* of turtles for a pond which has such a small *amount* of water.

An   See **A.**

And etc.   The *and* is unnecessary; *etc.* means *and so forth* (literally, *et cetera*, "and other things").

Antecedent   A word to which a pronoun refers.

> antecedent   pronoun
>   ↓   ↓
> When the ballet *dancers* appeared, *they* were dressed in pink.

Anyplace   Prefer *anywhere.*

Anyways   Prefer *anyway.*

Anywheres   Prefer *anywhere.*

Appositive   A word, phrase, or clause used as a noun and placed beside another word to explain it.

> appositive
>   ↓
> The *poet John Milton* wrote *Paradise Lost* while he was blind.

Article   *A* and *an* are indefinite articles; *the* is the definite article.

As   Weak in the sense of *because:*

> The client collected the full amount of insurance *as* his car ran off the cliff and was totally demolished.

Auxiliary verb   A verb used to help another verb indicate tense, mood, or voice. Principal auxiliaries are forms of the verbs *be* and *do.*

I *am* studying.
I *was* told to be ready by noon.
I *do* not think so.
I *shall* be there next week.
He *may* lose his job.

Awful A trite and feeble substitute for such words as *bad, shocking, ludicrous, ugly.*

Awhile, a while *Awhile* is an adverb; *a while* is an article and a noun.

> Stay *awhile.*
> Wait here for *a while.*

Bad, badly See page 43.

Because See **Reason is because.**

Being as, being that Use *because* or *since.*

Beside, besides *Beside* means *by the side of, next to; besides* means *in addition to.*

> Mr. Potts was sitting *beside* the stove.
> No one was in the room *besides* Mr. Potts.

Between See **Among.**

Between you and I Affectation for *between you and me.*

Bring, take *Bring* denotes motion toward the speaker. *Take* denotes motion away from the speaker.

> *Bring* me the hammer and *take* the saw to him.
> NOT *Bring* the saw to him.

Bust, busted Slang as forms of *burst. Bursted* is also unacceptable.

But, hardly, only, scarcely Preferably not used with another negative.

AVOID	PREFER
did not have but one	had but one, had only one
can't help but realize	can't help realizing
can't hardly realize	can hardly realize
wasn't there only two weeks	was there only two weeks
did not have scarcely enough	had scarcely enough

Can, may   In formal English, *can* is still used to denote ability; *may*, to denote permission. Informally the two are interchangeable.

FORMAL   *May* (not *can*) I go?

Cannot hardly, can't hardly   Double negatives. See **But, hardly, only, scarcely.**

Cannot help but, can't help but   Double negatives. See **But, hardly, only, scarcely.**

Capital, capitol   *Capitol* designates a building which is a seat of government; *capital* is used for all other meanings.

Case   English has remnants of three cases: subjective, possessive, and objective. Nouns are inflected for case only in the possessive (*father, father's*). An alternative way to show possession is with the "*of* phrase" (*the house, of the house*). Some pronouns, notably the personal pronouns and the relative pronoun *who*, are still fully inflected for three cases:

SUBJECTIVE (acting)   I, he, she, we, they, who

POSSESSIVE (possessing)   my (mine), your (yours), his, her (hers), its, our (ours), their (theirs), whose

OBJECTIVE (acted upon)   me, him, her, us, them, whom

Center around   Illogical. Use *center in* (or *on*) or *cluster around*.

Clause A group of words containing a subject and a predicate. See **Independent clause** and **Dependent clause.**

Climactic, climatic *Climactic* pertains to a climax; *climatic* pertains to climate.

Collective noun A word identifying a class or a group of persons or things.

Compare to, compare with After *compare* in similes, use *to;* in analyses of similarities and differences, use *with.*

> He *compared* the wrecked train *to* strewn and broken matches.
>
> He *compared* this train wreck *with* the one that occurred a month ago.

Complected Dialectal or colloquial. Use *complexioned.*

Complement A word or group of words used to complete a predicate. Predicate adjectives, predicate nominatives, direct objects, and indirect objects are complements.

Complement, compliment *To complement* means *to complete; to compliment* means *to praise.*

Complex, compound sentences A *complex sentence* has one independent clause and at least one dependent clause. A *compound sentence* has at least two independent clauses. A *compound-complex sentence* has at least two independent clauses and one dependent clause.

Conjunction A word used to connect sentences or sentence parts. See also **Coordinating conjunctions** and **Subordinating conjunctions.**

Conjunctive adverbs Adverbs used to relate two independent clauses which are separated by a semicolon: *however, therefore, moreover, then, consequently, besides,* etc. See §22a.

Considerable Basically an adjective, though used informally as a noun.

> STANDARD He had a *considerable* influence on his students.

> INFORMAL He made *considerable* each week.

Contemptible, contemptuous *Contemptible* means *deserving of scorn; contemptuous* means *feeling scorn.*

> The sophomore who was *contemptuous* toward freshmen was *contemptible.*

Continual, continuous *Continual* refers to a prolonged and rapid succession; *continuous* refers to an uninterrupted succession.

Coordinating conjunctions The simple conjunctions which join sentences and sentence parts of equal rank: *and, but, or, nor, for, yet, so.*

Correlative conjunctions Conjunctions used in pairs to join coordinate sentence parts. The most common are *either — or, neither — nor, not only — but also, both — and.*

Could of See **Of.**

Cute Informal and overused for such expressions as *pretty, dainty, attractive.*

Data See §7e.

Deal Informal and overused for *bargain, transaction,* or *business arrangement.* In *big deal,* slang.

Demonstrative adjectives and pronouns Words used to point out: *this, that, these, those.*

Dependent (subordinate) clause A group of words which contains both a subject and a predicate but which does not stand alone as a sentence. A dependent clause is frequently signaled by a subordinator (*who, which, what, that, since, because,* etc.) and always serves an adjective, noun, or adverb function.

ADJECTIVE	The tenor *who sang the aria* had just arrived from Italy.
NOUN	The critics agreed *that the young tenor had a magnificent voice.*
ADVERB	*When he sang,* even the sophisticated audience was enraptured.

Differ from, differ with   *Differ from* expresses unlikeness; *differ with* expresses disagreement.

> The twins *differ from* each other in personality.
> The twins *differ with* each other about politics.

Direct object   A noun, pronoun, or other substantive receiving the action of the verb.

> The angler finally caught the old trout.

Done   Past participle of *do.* Not to be used in place of *did,* as the past tense of *do:* "He *did* it," not "He *done* it."

Don't   Contraction of *do not;* not to be used for *doesn't,* the contraction of *does not.*

> He *doesn't.*
> NOT He *don't.*

Effect   See **Affect.**

Elliptical clause   A clause in which one or more words are understood.

>   *understood*
>   ↓
> The director admired no one else as much as (*he admired* or *he did*) her.

Enthused   Use *enthusiastic* in formal writing.

Etc.   See **And etc.**

Ever, every Use *every* in *every other, everybody, every now and then;* use *ever* in *ever and anon, ever so humble.*

Every day, everyday *Every day* is used as an adverb; *everyday*, as an adjective.

> He comes to look at the same picture in the gallery *every day*.
> His trip to the gallery is an *everyday* occurrence.

Exam Informal. Use *examination* in formal writing.

Except See **Accept.**

Expect Informal for *believe, suspect, think, suppose,* etc.

Expletive See §**7h.**

Fantastic Informal for *extraordinarily good.*

Farther, further Generally interchangeable, though many persons prefer *farther* in expressions of physical distance and *further* in expressions of time, quantity, and degree.

> My car used less gasoline and went *farther* than his.
> The second speaker went *further* into the issues than the first.

Fewer, less Use *fewer* to denote number; *less*, to denote amount or degree.

> With *fewer* advertisers, there will be *less* income from advertising.

Fine Often a poor substitute for a more exact word of approval or commendation.

Fix Informal for the noun *predicament.*

Flunk Informal. Prefer *fail* or *failure* in formal usage.

Folks Informal for *family* or *relatives.*

Funny Informal for *strange, remarkable,* or *peculiar.*

Further See **Farther.**

Gerund See **Verbal.**

Good Incorrect as an adverb. See page 42.

Grand Often vaguely used in place of more exact words like *majestic, magnificent, imposing.*

Had of Use *had.*

> I wish I *had* (not *had of*) known he was going.

Had ought Use *should.*

Hadn't ought Use *shouldn't.*

Hang, hanged, hung See page 10.

Hardly. See **But, hardly, only, scarcely.**

Has got, have got Use simply *has* or *have.*

Himself See **Myself.**

Illusion See **Allusion.**

Imply, infer *Imply* means to hint or suggest; *infer* means to draw a conclusion.

> The speaker *implied* that Mr. Falkner was guilty.
> The audience *inferred* that Mr. Falkner was guilty.

In, into *Into* denotes motion from the outside to the inside; *in* denotes position (enclosure).

> The lion was *in* the cage when the trainer walked *into* the tent.

Indefinite pronouns Pronouns not pointing out a particular person or thing. Some of the most common are *some, any, each, every, everyone, everybody, any, anyone, anybody, one,* and *neither.*

Independent (main) clause A group of words which contains a subject and a predicate and which grammatically can stand alone as a sentence.

Indirect object A word which indirectly receives the action of the verb.

> The actress wrote the *soldier* a letter.

Usually *to* or *for* is implied before the indirect object.

> The actress wrote (to) the *soldier* a letter.

Infer See **Imply.**

Infinitive See **Verbal.**

In regards to Unidiomatic. Use *in regard to* or *with regard to.*

Intensive pronouns Pronouns ending in *-self* and used for emphasis.

> The director *himself* will act the part of Hamlet.

Interjection A word used to exclaim or to express a strong emotion. It has no grammatical connections within its sentence. Some of the most common interjections are *oh, ah,* and *ouch.*

Interrogative pronouns See §9i.

Into See **In.**

Intransitive verb See **Voice.**

Irregardless Nonstandard for *regardless.*

Is when, is where Ungrammatical use of adverbial clause after a linking verb. Often misused in definitions and explanations.

NONSTANDARD Combustion *is when* (or *is where*) oxygen unites with other elements.

STANDARD Combustion occurs when oxygen unites with other elements.

STANDARD Combustion is a union of oxygen with other elements.

Its, it's   *Its* is the possessive case of the pronoun *it; it's* is a contraction of *it is.*

> *It's* exciting to parents when their baby cuts *its* first tooth.

Kind of, sort of   Informal as adverbs. Use *rather, somewhat,* etc.

COLLOQUIAL	Mr. Josephson was *sort of* disgusted.
FORMAL	Mr. Josephson was *rather* disgusted.
FORMAL (not an adverb)	What *sort of* book is that?

Kind of a, sort of a   Delete the *a;* use *kind of* and *sort of.*

> What *kind of* (not *kind of a*) pipe do you smoke?

Lay, lie   See pages 11, 12.

Learn, teach   *Learn* means *to acquire knowledge. Teach* means *to impart knowledge.*

> He could not *learn* how to work the problem until Mr. Smithers *taught* him the formula.

Less   See **Fewer.**

Liable   See **Likely.**

Lie   See pages 11, 12.

Like   Prefer *like* as a preposition; prefer *as, as if,* or *as though* as a conjunction.

CONJUNCTION	She acted *as if* she had never been on the stage before.
PREPOSITION	She acted *like* a novice.
CONJUNCTION	She acted *like* she had never had a date before. (Not preferred.)

Such popular phrases as "like it is" derive part of their appeal from their lighthearted defiance of convention.

Likely, liable Use *likely* to express probability; use *liable* to express responsibility or obligation, often with legal connotations.

> You are *likely* to have an accident if you drive recklessly.
> Since your father owns the car, he will be *liable* for damages.

Linking verb A verb which does not express action but links the subject to another word which names or describes it. See §10c. Common linking verbs are *be, become,* and *seem.*

Loose A frequent misspelling of *lose. Loose* is an adjective; *lose* is a verb.

> She wore a *loose* and trailing gown.
> Speculators often *lose* their money.

Lot of, lots of Informal in the sense of *much, many, a great deal.*

May See **Can.**

May of See **Of.**

Might of See **Of.**

Modifier A word (or word group) which limits or describes another word. See **Adjective** and **Adverb.**

Mood The mood (or mode) of a verb indicates whether an action is to be thought of as fact, command, wish, or condition contrary to fact. Modern English has three moods.

INDICATIVE for ordinary statements and questions
> *Does* she play the guitar?
> She *does.*

IMPERATIVE for ordinary commands and entreaty
> *Stay* with me.
> *Let* him stay.
> *Let* us pray.

The imperative is formed like the plural present indicative, without *-s.*

SUBJUNCTIVE in certain idiomatic expressions of wish, command, or condition contrary to fact

> If I *were* you. . . .
> I move that the meeting *be* adjourned.
> It is necessary that he *stay* absolutely quiet.
> I wish he *were* going with you.
> If this *be* true, no man ever loved.

The commonest subjunctive forms are *were* and *be.* All others are formed like the present-tense plural form without *-s.*

Most Informal for *almost* in such expressions as the following.

> He is late for class *almost* (not *most*) every day.

Must of See **Of.**

Myself, yourself, himself These words are reflexives or intensives, not strict equivalents of *I, me, you, he, him.*

INTENSIVE I *myself* helped Father cut the wheat.
  I helped Father cut the wheat *myself.*

REFLEXIVE I cut *myself.*

NOT Give it to *myself.*

LOOSE The elopement was known only to Sherry and *myself.*
  Only Kay and *myself* had access to the safe.

PREFERRED The elopement was known only to Sherry and *me.*
  Only Kay and *I* had access to the safe.

Nice A weak substitute for more exact words like *attractive, modest, pleasant, kind,* etc.

Nominative case See **Case.**

Noun   A word which names and which has gender, number, and case. There are proper nouns, which name particular people, places, or things (*Thomas Jefferson, Paris*, the *Colosseum*); common nouns, which name one or more of a group (*alligator, high school, politician*); collective nouns (see §**7d** and §**8c**); abstract nouns, which name ideas, feelings, beliefs, etc. (*religion, justice, dislike, enthusiasm*); concrete nouns, which name things perceived through the senses (*lemon, hatchet, worm*).

Noun clause   See **Dependent clause.**

Nowheres   Dialectal. Use *nowhere.*

Number   See **Amount.**

Object of preposition   See **Preposition** and §**9b.**

Objective case   See **Case.**

Obsolete words   Not used in modern English. Examples: *jump* for "exactly," and *shrewd* in the sense of "bad" or "evil."

Of   Avoid phrases like *might of, may of, could of, would of, should of*, etc. Use *might have*, etc.

Off of   *Off* is sufficient.

> He fell *off* (not *off of*) the water tower.

On a whole   Confusion of two constructions, *as a whole* and *on the whole.*

Only   See **But, hardly, only, scarcely.**

Ought to of   See **Of.**

Participle   See **Verbal.**

Parts of speech   The parts of speech are noun, pronoun, adjective, verb, adverb, conjunction, interjection, preposition. See each of these in this glossary.

Party   Informal when used to mean *person*, except in legal usage.

Percent, per cent Use after figures, as "three *percent*," "50 *percent*." Do not use for *percentage:*

> Only a small *percentage* (not *percent*) of the men had degrees.

Personal pronouns Words like *I, you, he, she, it, we, they, mine, yours, his, hers, its, ours, theirs.*

Phenomena Plural. The singular is *phenomenon.*

Phrase A group of closely related words which do not contain both a subject and a predicate. There are subject phrases (*The new drill sergeant* was young), verb phrases (*should have been*), verbal phrases (*climbing high mountains*), prepositional phrases (see **Preposition**), appositive phrases (my brother, *the black sheep of the family*), etc.

Plenty Informal when used as an adverb.

> INFORMAL He was *plenty* sick.
>
> FORMAL He was *very* sick.

P.M. See **A.M.**

Predicate The verb in a clause (simple predicate) or the verb and its modifiers, complements, and objects (complete predicate).

Predicate adjective An adjective following a linking verb and describing the subject.

> The rose is *artificial.*

See §**10c.**

Predicate complement See **Complement.**

Predicate nominative See **Subjective complement.**

Predominate, predominant Do not use the verb *predominate* for the adjective *predominant.*

Preposition   A connective which joins a noun or a pronoun to the rest of a sentence. A prepositional phrase may be used as either an adjective or an adverb.

ADJECTIVE   Joseph wore a coat *of many colors.*

ADVERB   He leadeth me *beside the still waters.*

Principal, principle   Use *principal* to mean *the chief* or *most important.* Use *principle* to mean *a rule* or *a truth.*

> The *principal* reason for her delinquency was never discussed.
> The *principal* of Brookwood High School resigned.
> To act without *principle* leads to delinquency.

Pronominal adjective   An adjective which is the possessive form of a pronoun (*my* book, *their* enthusiasm).

Pronoun   A word which stands for a noun. See **Personal pronouns, Demonstrative adjectives and pronouns, Reflexive pronouns, Intensive pronouns, Interrogative pronouns, Indefinite pronouns,** and **Relative pronouns.**

Quite   Do not confuse the spelling of *quite* and *quiet.*

Quote   A verb. Prefer *quotation* as a noun.

Raise, rise   See page 11.

Real   Informal or dialectal as an adverb meaning *really* or *very.*

Reason is (was) because   Especially in writing, do not use for *the reason is that. Because* should introduce an adverbial clause, not a noun clause used as a predicate nominative.

NOT   The *reason* Abernathy enlisted *was because* he failed in college.

BUT   The *reason* Abernathy enlisted *was that* he failed in college.

OR   Abernathy enlisted *because* he failed in college.

Reflexive pronouns   Pronouns ending in *-self* and indicating that the subject acts upon itself.

   The butcher cut *himself.*

Relative pronouns   See §9i and **Myself.**

Respectfully, respectively   *Respectfully* means with *respect;* *respectively* means *each in the order given.*

   He *respectfully* thanked the president for his diploma.

   Crossing the platform, he passed *respectively* by the speaker, the dean, and the registrar.

Right   Dialectal for *very* or *somewhat,* as in the expression "*right* tired."

Said   Not to be used in the sense of *previously mentioned,* except in a legal context (as in "The *said* object was found in the room of the accused").

Same   Rarely used as a pronoun unless it is preceded by *the,* except in legal style (as in "Drinking by minors is illegal and *same* shall result in arrest").

Scarcely   See **But, hardly, only, scarcely.**

Sensual, sensuous   *Sensual* connotes gross bodily pleasures; *sensuous* refers favorably to what is experienced through the senses.

Set, sit   See pages 11, 12.

Shall, will In strictly formal English, to indicate simple futurity, *shall* is conventional in the first person (I *shall*, we *shall*); *will*, in the second and third persons (you *will*, he *will*, they *will*). To indicate determination, duty, or necessity, *will* is formal in the first person (I *will*, we *will*); *shall*, in the second and third persons (you *shall*, he *shall*, they *shall*). These distinctions are weaker than they used to be, and *will* is increasingly used in all persons.

Should of See **Of.**

Simple sentence A sentence consisting only of one independent clause.

So For the use of *so* in incomplete constructions, see page 52. The use of *so* for *so that* sometimes causes confusion.

Someplace Prefer *somewhere.*

Sometime, some time *Sometime* is used adverbially to designate an indefinite point of time. *Some time* refers to a period or duration of time.

> I will see you *sometime* next week.
> I have not seen him for *some time.*

Somewheres Dialectal for *somewhere.*

Sort of See **Kind of.**

Sort of a See **Kind of a.**

Subject A word or group of words about which the sentence or clause makes a statement.

SIMPLE SUBJECT *Whitman* left the lecture on astronomy.

COMPOUND SUBJECT *Whitman* and *Emerson* were transcendentalists.

CLAUSE AS SUBJECT *That Whitman left the lecture on astronomy* is well known.

Subjective case **See Case.**

Subjective complement   A word or group of words which follows a linking verb and identifies the subject.

> This book is a best-selling historical *novel*.
> His excuse was *that he had been sick*.

Subordinate clause   **See Dependent clause.**

Subordinating conjunctions   Conjunctions which join sentence parts of unequal rank. Most frequently they begin dependent clauses. Some common subordinating conjunctions are *because, since, though, although, if, when, while, before, after, as, until, so that, as long as, as if, where, unless, as soon as, whereas, in order that.*

Sure   Informal as an adverb for *surely, certainly.*

> INFORMAL   The speaker *sure* criticized his opponent.
>
> FORMAL   The speaker *certainly* criticized his opponent.

Sure and, try and   Use *sure to, try to.*

> Be *sure to* (not *and*) notice the costumes of the Hungarian folk dancers.

Suspicion   Avoid as a verb. Use *suspect.*

Swell   Slang or informal for *good;* often vaguely used for more exact words of approval.

Teach   **See Learn.**

Terrible   Often a poor substitute for a more exact word.

Their, there   Not interchangeable. *Their* is the possessive of *they; there* is either an adverb meaning *in that place* or an expletive ("There is. . . ." "There are. . . .").

> *Their* dachshund is sick.
> *There* is a veterinarian's office in this block. (Expletive.)
> *There* it is on the corner. (Adverb of place.)

These (those) kind, these (those) sort   *These (those)* is plural; *kind (sort)* is singular. Therefore use *this (that) kind, this (that) sort; these (those) kinds, these (those) sorts.*

Thusly   Prefer *thus.*

Transitive verb   See **Voice.**

Try and   See **Sure and.**

Unique   Means *one of a kind;* hence it may not logically be compared. *Unique* should not be loosely used for *unusual* or *strange.*

Use   Sometimes carelessly written for the past tense, *used.*

> Thomas Jefferson *used* (not *use*) to bathe in cold water almost every morning.

Verb   A word or group of words expressing action, being, or state of being.

> Othello *killed* Desdemona.
> What *is* man?
> I *shall have returned.*
> The fire *has been built.*

Verbal   A word derived from a verb and used as a noun, an adjective, or an adverb. A verbal may be a gerund, a participle, or an infinitive.

GERUND   1. ends in *-ing*
2. is used as a noun

> *gerund*   *object of gerund*
> ↓   ↓
> *Shoeing horses* is almost a lost art.
> ↑
> *gerund phrase, used as subject*

PARTICIPLE
1. ends in *-ing, -ed, -d, -t, -n,* etc.
2. is used as an adjective

prepositional phrase, modifying participle

participle

Riding at top speed, he snatched the child from danger.

participial phrase, modifying subject

INFINITIVE
1. begins with *to,* which may be understood
2. is used as an adjective, an adverb, or a noun

infinitive   *object of infinitive*

To rescue the child this way was a difficult feat.

infinitive phrase, used as subject

infinitive, used as adjective

Black Beauty is a good book *to read* to a child.

infinitive, used as adverb

He was eager *to ride* his new horse.

Verb phrase   See **Phrase.**

Voice   Transitive verbs have two forms to show whether their subjects act (active voice) or are acted upon (passive voice). See §**5.**

Wait on   Unidiomatic for *wait for. Wait on* correctly means *to serve.*

Ways   Prefer *way* when designating a distance.

A long *way* (instead of "A long *ways*")

When, where   See **Is when, is where.**

Where   Do not misuse for *that.*

> I read in the newspaper *that* (not *where*) you saved a child's life.

Where at   The *at* is unnecessary.

> NOT   *Where* is he *at?*
> BUT   *Where* is he?

While   Do not overuse for such other conjunctions as *but*, *and*, *whereas*, and *although*.

Whose, who's   *Whose* is the possessive of *who; who's* is a contraction of *who is.*

-wise   A suffix overused in combinations with nouns, such as *budget-wise, progress-wise,* and *business-wise.*

Without   Dialectal for *unless*, as in "I cannot come *without* you pay for the ticket."

Would of   See **Of.**

Index

Abbreviations Often Used in Marking Student Papers *(numerals refer to page numbers)*

DATE DUE

NOV 3 0 1997	